Best Wishes

Captain Alan Phillips
Royal Navy

HMS ENDURANCE
1994

FOREWORD
by Admiral of the Fleet
HRH The Prince Philip, Duke of Edinburgh K.G., K.T., O.M., G.B.E.

It doesn't take many years of peace and the absence of a threat of invasion for people to forget that it is the armed services which gained that security and remain its only guarantee.

For 1,000 years the Navy has been called upon again and again to defend the freedom and independence of the people of the British Isles. Many volumes have been written about our maritime history but pictures can often say more than words. The illustrations in this book tell the story in a vivid and evocative manner which, I am sure, will help the reader to visualise the great moments in the long history of the Royal Navy.

Almost the best thing about this book is that it will generate considerable income for King George's Fund for Sailors. As I am President of the Fund I am naturally hoping that the book will attract a great many readers.

King George's Fund for Sailors wishes to acknowledge the generosity and interest of the following organisations without whose help the publication of "The Royal Navy — 1,000 Years of Peace and War" would not have been possible.

A

Abbey National Building Society 26
Abbey House, Baker Street, London NW1 6XL

Airtech Ltd 133
Haddenham, Aylesbury, Bucks HP17 8JD

Alcan Plate Ltd 78
PO Box 383, Kitts Green, Birmingham B33 9QR

The Alexandra Towing Co Ltd 28
Castle Chambers, 43 Castle Street, Liverpool L2 9TA

Allied-Lyons plc 64
156 St. John Street, London EC1P 1AR

ANZ Merchant Bank Ltd 30
65 Holborn Viaduct, London EC1A 2EU

Associated Fisheries plc 53
16 Queen Anne's Gate, London SW1H 9AQ

The Associated Octel Co Ltd 72
20 Berkeley Square, London W1X 6DT

B

Babcock International plc 32
Cleveland House, St. James's Square, London SW1Y 4LN

Bain & Co (Securities) Ltd 61
115 Houndsditch, London EC3A 7BU

J. C. Bamford Excavators Ltd 10
Rocester, Staffs. S14 5JP

Bank of New Zealand 61
BNZ House, 91 Gresham Street, London EC2V 7BL

Barclays Bank plc 9
54 Lombard Street, London EC3P 4AH

Bass plc 24
30 Portland Place, London W1N 3DF

Beaufort Air-Sea Equipment Ltd 116
Beaufort Road, Birkenhead L41 1HQ

Belfast Car Ferries Ltd 47
47 Donnegall Quay, Belfast BT1 3ED

The Rowan Bentall Charity Trust 43
Wood Street, Kingston-upon-Thames KT1 1TX

Bird's Eye Walls Ltd 38
Walton Court, Station Avenue, Walton-on-Thames KT12 1NT

Birmal Castings Ltd 43
Dartmouth Road, Smethwick, Warley

Bonar Bray Ltd 130
Britannia Road, Waltham Cross EN8 3PB

C. T. Bowring & Co Ltd 62
The Bowring Building, Tower Place, London EC3P 3BE

BPB Industries plc 18
Langley Park House, Uxbridge Road, Slough SL3 6DU

Brent Walker Holdings plc & The Brighton Marina Co Ltd 70
197 Knightsbridge, London SW7 1RB

British Aerospace plc 65
100 Pall Mall, London SW1Y 5HR

British & Commonwealth Shipping Co plc & The Bristow Helicopter Group 93
Cayzer House, 2 & 4 St. Mary Axe, London EC3A 8BP

British Manufacturers & Research Co Ltd 75
Springfield Road, Grantham, Lincs.

British Telecommunications plc 106
81 Newgate St., London EC1A 7AJ

Brock's Fireworks Ltd 37
Sanquhar, Dumfriesshire DG4 6JP

David Brown Gear Industries Ltd 107
Park Gear Works, Huddersfield HD4 5DD

James Buchanan & Co Ltd 48
3 St. James's Square, London SW1

H. P. Bulmer Holdings plc 59
Cider Mills, Plough Lane, Hereford HR4 0LF

The Burmah Oil Co plc 131
Burmah House, Pipers Way, Swindon SN3 1RE

C

Calor Gas Ltd 90
Appleton Park, Slough SL1 7UG

Champion Sparking Plug Co Ltd 13
Arrowebrook Road, Upton, Wirral L49 0UQ

J. S. Chinn Holdings Ltd 40
Coventry Road, Exhall, Coventry CV7 9FT

City of London 79
Guildhall, London EC2P 2EJ

City of Portsmouth 25
Guildhall, Guildhall Square, Portsmouth PO1 2AD

CJB Developments Ltd 118
Airport Service Road, Portsmouth PO3 5PG

Clyde Port Authority 48
16 Robertson Street, Glasgow G2 8DS

Coats Viyella plc 76
Bank House, Charlotte Street, Manchester M1 4FT

Constantine Holdings Ltd 23
10 Grafton Street, London W1X 3LA

Henry Cooch Ltd 74
PO Box 40, Sevenoaks, Kent TN15 8LN

Coopers & Lybrand & Associates 14
Plumtree Court, London EC4 4HT

Cosalt plc 33
Fish Dock Road, Grimsby DK31 3NW

Coubro PTC National plc 92
430 Barking Road, Plaistow, London E13 8HJ

Crane Packing Ltd 126
Crossbow House, 40 Liverpool Road, Slough SL1 4QX

Crouzet Ltd 44
Hawley Lane, Farnborough, Hants GU14 8HY

Cunard Steamship Co Ltd 110
1 Berkeley Street, London W1X 6NN

D

W. A. Dawson Ltd 25
Sundon Park, Luton, Beds. LU3 3AB

Delta Group plc 12
Greets Green Road, West Bromwich B70 9ER

Didsbury Engineering Co Ltd 133
Clifton Works, Manor Road, Manchester M19 3EJ

Doncasters Monk Bridge Ltd 125
Whitehall Road, Leeds LS1

Dowty Group plc 139
Cheltenham GL51 0TP

Richard Dunston (Hessle) Ltd 84
Haven Shipyard, Hessle, Nr. Humberside HU13 0EA

E

Electro Dynamic Construction Co Ltd 49
Station App., St. Mary Cray, Orpington BR5 2ND

Engelhard Ltd 96
Davis Road, Chessington, Surrey KT9 1TD

Ernst & Whinney 34
Becket House, 1 Lambeth Palace Road, London SE1 7EU

Esso UK plc 91
Esso House, Victoria Street, London SW1E 5JW

F

Fairey Holdings Ltd 57
Cranford Lane, Heston, Hounslow TW5 9NQ

Ferranti plc 8
Bridge House, Park Road, Gatley, Cheadle, Ches. SK8 4HZ

Findus Ltd 95
St. George's House, Croydon, Surrey CR9 1NR

Fisher Controls Ltd 123
Century Works, Lewisham, London SE13 7LN

Flight Refuelling Ltd 74
Brook Road, Wimborne, Dorset BH21 2BJ

Furness Withy Agency Ltd 26
Furness House, Canute Road, Southampton SO1 1AA

G

Gallaher Ltd 71
65 Kingsway, London WC1

Gallic Shipping Ltd 43
Blomfield House, 85 London Wall, London EC2M 7AD

GEC Avionics Ltd 115
Airport Works, Rochester, Kent ME1 2XX

Geest Holdings Ltd 23
White House Chambers, Albion Springs, Spalding, Lincs P11 2AL

Gibraltar Shiprepair Ltd 21
The Dockyard, Gibraltar

Godiva Fire Pumps Ltd 117
Charles Street, Warwick CV3 5LR

Grand Metropolitan plc 67
11-12 Hanover Square, London W1A 1DP

Graseby Dynamics Ltd 80
Park Avenue, Bushey, Watford, Herts WD2 2BW

Guinness plc 137
39 Portman Square, London W1H 9HB

H

Halmatic Ltd 94
Osborne Rescue Boats Ltd
Brookside Road, Havant, Hants PO9 1JR

Harland and Wolff plc 105
Queen's Island, Belfast BT3 3DU

Harrisons (Clyde) Ltd 48
16-17 Woodside Crescent, Glasgow G3 7UT

Harrisons & Crosfield plc 81
1-4 Great Tower Street, London EC3R 5AB

Harveys of Bristol Ltd 132
Harvey House, 12 Denmark Street, Bristol BS15 DQ

Hawker Siddeley Group plc 103
18 St. James's Square, London SW1Y 4LJ

Hays Space Technology Ltd 132
Hays House, Steepledrive, Alton, Hants GU34 1TN

C. E. Heath plc 52
Cuthbert Heath House, 150 The Minories, London EC3N 1NR

Henderson Administration Ltd 24
26 Finsbury Square, London EC2A 1DA

Herd & Mackenzie Ltd 76
Commercial Road, Buckie AB5 1UR

Hewlett-Packard Ltd 35
King Street Lane, Winnersh, Wokingham RG11 5AR

Jane Hodge Foundation 63
31 Windsor Place, Cardiff CF1 3UR

Honeywell Leafield Ltd 49
Leafield, Corsham, Wilts SN13 9SS

Hotspur Armoured Products Division — Penman Eng Ltd 112
Heath Hall, Dumfriesshire DG1 3NY

Hunting Engineering Ltd 19
Reddingswood, Ampthill, Bedford MK45 2HD

I

IAL plc 74
Aeradio House, Hayes Road, Southall, Middlesex UB2 5NJ

IBM United Kingdom Ltd 13
IBM South Bank, 76 Upper Ground, London SE1 9PZ

ICL Defence Systems Ltd 100
322 Euston Road, London NW1 3BD

IMI Summerfield Ltd 82
Kidderminster, Worcs DY11 7RZ

IMI Yorkshire Alloys Ltd 111
PO Box 166, Leeds LS1 1RD

Imperial Chemical Industries plc 129
'Perspex' Division, Orchard Mill, Melrose Street, Darwen, Lancs BB31 0QB

Inco Engineered Products Ltd 87
Wiggin Street, Birmingham B16 0AJ

Industria Engineering Products Ltd 117
Eskdale Road, Uxbridge UB8 2SL

J

Jane's Publishing Co Ltd 135
238 City Road, London EC1

Johnson Wax Ltd 12
Frimley Green, Camberley, Surrey GU16 5AJ

K

The Walter Kidde Co Ltd 84
Belvue Road, Northolt UB5 6QW

Knight Frank & Rutley 49
20 Hanover Square, London W1A 0AH

L

Lang Brothers Ltd 77
100 West Nile Street, Glasgow G12 QT

Leslie & Godwin Ltd 58
6 Braham Street, London E1 8ED

Charles Letts & Co Ltd 12
Diary House, Borough Road, London SE1 1DW

The Lingard Group inc. Mediscus Products Ltd 96
Westminster Road, Wareham, Dorset BH20 4SP

Lloyds Bank plc 46
71 Lombard Street, London EC3P 3BS

Lloyds Register of Shipping 84
71 Fenchurch Street, London EC3M 4BS

Lucas Aerospace Ltd 109
Brueton House, New Road, Solihull B91 3JX

M

MacTaggart, Scott & Co Ltd 101
PO Box 1, Hunter Avenue, Loanhead, Nr. Edinburgh EH20 5SP

Marconi Communications Systems Ltd 80
Marconi House, New Street, Chelmsford CM1 1PL

Marconi Space & Defence Systems Ltd 97
The Grove, Warren Lane, Stanmore HA7 4LY

Marks & Spencer plc 99
Michael House, 37-67 Baker Street, London W1A 1DN

Mark Tyzack & Sons Ltd 13
PO Box 103, 200 Carwood Road, Sheffield S4 7LQ

J. Marr & Son Ltd 113
St. Andrew's Dock, Hull HU3 4PL

Mathew Hall plc 66
Mathew Hall House, 7 Baker Street, London W1M 1AB

MEL Ltd 120
Manor Royal, Crawley, West Sussex RH10 2PE

Metallisation Service Ltd 66
Pear Tree Lane, Dudley DY2 0XH

Metoptic Engineering Ltd 42
22 Woodcock Industrial Estate, Warminster BA12 9DX

MMM Consultancy Group 47
Handmills Road, Basingstoke RG21 2XN

Mobil Holdings Ltd 51
Mobil House, Victoria Street, London SW1E 6QB

Motorola Military & Aerospace Ltd 59
Taylors Road, Hitchin, Herts.

MSA (Britain) Ltd 82
East Shawhead, Coatbridge ML5 4TD

N

National Westminster Bank plc 89
41 Lothbury, London EC2P 2BP

Louis Newmark plc 104
15 Ormside Way, Redhill RH1 2QA

Niarchos (London) Ltd 54
41 Park Street, London W1

Norcros plc 26
Spencers Wood, Reading RG7 1NT

O

Ocean Transport & Trading plc 20
India Buildings, Water Street, Liverpool L20 RB

P

Pandect Group Ltd 42
Wellington Road, High Wycombe, Bucks

Paxman Engines Ltd 132
PO Box 8, Standard Works, Colchester, Essex

Pearl Assurance plc 58
252 High Holborn, London WC1V 7EB

Peat, Marwick, McLintock & Co 61
1 Puddledock, Blackfriars, London EC4V 3PD

Peninsula & Oriental Steam Navigation Co Ltd 122
Liscartan House, 127 Sloane Street, London SW1X 9BA

Petrofina (UK) Ltd 16
Petrofina House, 1 Ashley Avenue, Epsom KT18 5AD

Pilkington Brothers plc 27
Prescot Road, St. Helens, Merseyside WA10 3TT

Plessey Defence Systems Ltd 31
Grange Road, Christchurch, Dorset BH23 4JE

Plessey Naval Systems Ltd 128
Templecombe, Somerset BA3 0DH

Port of Felixstowe Ltd 36
European House, The Dock, Felixstowe IP11 8TB

Portsmouth & Sunderland Newspapers plc 114
Buckton House, 37 Abingdon Road, London W8 6AH

Precision Systems Ltd 123
Harding Way, Somersham Road, St. Ives, Cambs. PE17 4WR

Provident Mutual Life Assurance Association 119
25-31 Moorgate, London EC2R 6BA

Pussers Rum (Morgan Furze Ltd) 86
IDV Gilbey House, 4th Avenue, Harlow, Essex

R

Racal Group Services Ltd 127
21 Market Place, Wokingham, Berks RG11 1AJ

Raychem Ltd 83
Faraday Road, Dorcan, Swindon SN3 5HH

RCA Systems Ltd-Cerco Ltd 68
Lincoln Way, Windmill Road, Sunbury-on-Thames TW16 7HW

Rediffusion Radio Systems Ltd 35
Newton Road, Crawley, West Sussex RH10 2PY

RHP plc 121
PO Box 20, Pilgrim House, High Street, Billericay CM12 9XY

Rolls-Royce plc 136
65 Buckingham Gate, London SW1E 6AT

Rothmans International Ltd 96
Oxford Road, Aylesbury, Bucks

The Royal Bank of Scotland plc 29
42 St. Andrew's Square, Edinburgh EH2 2YE

S

Saccone & Speed International Ltd 138
21 Golden Square, London W1R 3PA

Serco Ltd 68
Lincoln Way, Windmill Road, Sunbury-on-Thames TW16 7HW

Christian Salvesen plc 108
50 East Fettes Avenue, Edinburgh EH4 1EQ

Schlumberger (Solartron) UK Ltd 66
Hays Wharf, Millmead, Guildford GU2 5HU

Securicor Group plc 58
20 Fulham Centre, London SW6

Serck Heat Transfer Ltd 130
Warwick Road, Birmingham B11 2QY

Shell Tankers (UK) Ltd 50
Shell Centre, London SE1 7PQ

Short Brothers Ltd 55
Airport Road, Belfast BT3 9DZ

Singer & Friedlander Ltd 11
21 New Street, Bishopsgate, London EC2M 4HR

S.I.R.S. Navigation Ltd 117
186a Milton Road, Swanscombe, Kent DA10 0LX

Smiths Industries Aerospace & Defence Systems Ltd 124
765 Finchley Road, London NW11 8DS

Spunalloys Ltd 80
Northcote Street, Walsall, West Midlands W52 8BJ

STC Defence Systems Ltd 123
Christchurch Way, Greenwich, London SE10 0AQ

Stone Boilers Ltd 134
PO Box 78, Tipton Road, Tividale, Warley, West Midlands

Bernard Sunley Charitable Trust 17
79 Park Street, London W1

Swan Hunter Shipbuilders Ltd 102
PO Box 1, Wallsend, Tyne & Wear NE28 6EQ

John Swire & Sons Ltd 85
Regis House, King William Street, London EC4R 9BE

Systems Designers plc 78
Systems House, 105 Fleet Road, Fleet GU13 8NZ

T

Tanqueray Gordon & Co Ltd 15
260 Goswell Road, London EC1V 7EE

Talbot Weaving Co Ltd 33
Talbot Mills, Chorley, Lancs

The Taunton Cider Co Ltd 47
Norton Fitzwarren, Taunton, Somerset TA2 6RP

Technitron Ltd 118
Doman Road, Camberley GU15 3DH

Texaco Overseas Tankships Ltd 60
195 Knightsbridge, London SW7 1RU

Thames Television Ltd 41
306 Euston Road, London NW1 3BB

Thorn EMI Electronics Ltd 88
Blyth Road, Hayes UB3 3JX

Tinsley Wire Industries Ltd 42
PO Box 119, Shepcote Lane, Sheffield S9 1TY

TNT Roadfreight UK Ltd 34
102 Long Street, Atherstone, Warks CV9 1BS

F. H. Tomkins plc 118 133
East Putney Hs, 84 Upper Richmond Rd, London SW15 2ST

Trago Mills Group Ltd 44
Twowatersfoot, Liskeard, Cornwall

Truflo Ltd 34
Westwood Road, Witton, Birmingham B6 7JF

Trusthouse Forte plc 59
86 Park Lane, London W1A 3AA

TVS/Television South Ltd 22
Television Centre, Vintners Park, Maidstone ME14 5NZ

Tyne Tees Television Ltd IFC & IBC
The TV Centre, Newcastle-upon-Tyne, NE1 2AL

U

United Rum Merchants Ltd 112
Prewetts Mill, Worthing Road, Horsham RH12 1SY

United Towing Ltd 111
Boston House, St. Andrew's Dock, Hull HU3 4PR

United Transport Co Ltd 33
5 Bury Street, London EC3

V

Vanguard Unit Trust Managers Ltd 73
65 Holborn Viaduct, London EC1A2 E11

Vega-Cantley 111
Unit J, Eskdale Road, Uxbridge.

Vickers plc 56
Vickers House, Millbank Tower, London SW1P 4RA

Vickers Shipbuilding & Engineering Ltd 98
Barrow Works, Barrow-in-Furness LA14 1AB

W

Watkins-Johnson Ltd 23
Dedworth Road, Oakley Green, Windsor SL4 4LH

Andrew Weir & Co Ltd — The Bank Line Ltd 45
Baltic Exchange Building, 19 Bury Street, London EC3A 5AU

Whessoe plc 78
Brinkburn Road, Darlington DL3 6DS

Wilkinson Sword Ltd 39
11-13 Brunel Road, London W3 7UH

Williams & James Ltd 82
Chequers Bridge, Gloucester GL1 4LL

Wimpey Marine Ltd 112
South Denes Road, Great Yarmouth NR30 6QQ

Woods of Colchester Ltd incorporating Keith Blackman 130
Tufnell Way, Colchester CO4 5AR

Woolwich Equitable Building Society 24
Equitable House, Woolwich SE18

Worshipful Company of Shipwrights 76
Ironmongers Hall, London EC2Y 8AA

Y

Yarrow Shipbuilders Ltd 140
South Street, Scotstoun, Glasgow G14 0XN

Yewlands Engineering Co Ltd 44
Fowler Road, Ilford IG6 3UT

York International Ltd 35
Gardiners Lane South, Basildon SS14 3HE

Young & Co's Brewery plc 69
The Ram Brewery, Wandsworth, London SW18 4JD

MINISTRY OF DEFENCE
MAIN BUILDING
WHITEHALL LONDON SW1A 2HB

CHIEF OF THE DEFENCE STAFF

A thousand years of naval history must also be, for a maritime nation, a thousand years of its own history. King Alfred's recognition of the necessity for seapower has been echoed down the centuries by all our rulers. Henry VII's big guns and stout ships initiated a supremacy which served well his descendants, Henry VIII and Elizabeth I, and laid the foundations of the glorious tradition that informs the pages of this splendid book.

We can also be proud of our naval record in preserving the freedom of the seas, charting the unknown, defeating slavery, and protecting trade from the depredations of pirates and the Sovereign's enemies. Innovation, whether it was the solution of the problem of longitude, the cure for scurvy, in naval aviation, or in the field of saturation diving, has always been a keynote.

But Royal or governmental patronage, however steadfast, avails this country nothing without the skill and courage of what the Royal Navy often calls "the greatest single factor", the seaman. We owe our seafaring people, both military and civilian, much, and while the brutalities of the eighteenth century are long gone, there still remains a need to care for our own when their seagoing careers are finished. In this, I admire the work of the King George's Fund for Sailors, and wish them and this book all the success they deserve.

KING GEORGE'S FUND FOR SAILORS

Incorporated under Royal Charter
Registered Charity No. 226446
1 CHESHAM STREET LONDON SW1X 8NF

KGFS
Patron HER MAJESTY THE QUEEN

President
Admiral of the Fleet
H.R.H. THE PRINCE PHILIP, DUKE OF EDINBURGH
KG, PC, KT, OM, GBE

Chairman of the General Council
Admiral SIR ANTHONY MORTON, GBE, KCB

Deputy Chairman
Captain SIR MILES WINGATE, KCVO

General Secretary
Captain KEITH SUTHERLAND, RN

Through the generosity of the publishers Messrs Seagull SA and the Companies and Organisations which have sponsored the pages in this book, all the proceeds from its sale come to King George's Fund for Sailors (KGFS), the Fund set up in 1917 for the relief of distress and poverty amongst Seafarers and their dependants. KGFS does this by securing and giving financial aid and support to those Charities which help such Seafaring or ex-Seafaring people.

In buying this book you acquire not only something of the greatest interest and the highest quality but also help the Fund to provide for the needs of the less fortunate Seafarers of our country, whether these be men or women, officers or ratings, Merchant Navy or Royal Navy or from the Fishing Fleet - or their dependants.

In the first 50 years of its existence the Fund distributed £8½ million to the Charities, Funds and Trusts which cared for Seafarers and their dependants.

Over the last 20 years the level of our annual support has built up steadily to a total of £11½ million and today, with our Grants approaching £1½ million every year, their calls for our help are increasing as those who have suffered the hazards of the sea, especially during the 1939-45 war, grow older.

Thank you - and all those who have made the publication of this book possible.

Acknowledgments

To give an impression of the great saga of human enterprise and material fact that a thousand years of the Royal Navy represents in the pages of a book such as this was acknowledged at its conception as being a task of research and selection as well as effective presentation, of formidable magnitude.

What must now be acknowledged is the equally great scale of the co-operation and generosity that was encountered during the course of this undertaking.

It is a pictorial record and immediately obvious are the contributions of the artists' outstanding and evocative work and especially the present day contributors — Robert Taylor (including the fine panorama of our history's latest great naval episode on the dustcover), John Hamilton and Michael Turner for making the Second World War come alive in these pages; Alan Fearney and John Worsley with his personal experience contribution as a POW. In addition to the most generous waiver of reproduction fees, these artists and others, particularly Pat Barnard of that Aladdin's Cave of military pictures, The Military Gallery, Bath; and Thomas Head, publisher of John Hamilton's book on the war at sea; have facilitated the selection process with their suggestions and advice. With less recent history, the Imperial War Museum through the help of Dr A Borg and J Simmons, before his well earned retirement, with his unrivalled mental inventory of that organisation's artworks, with Pauline Allwright and Jenny Wood (and Alan Williams of the Photographic Department) provided material for this period, as did their colleagues in the National Maritime Museum from whence the help of David Cordingly, Joan Moore and her successor Ann Carvel are gratefully acknowledged, together with other organisations including The Mary Rose Trust, Capt Charles Dowds RN; The Warrior Trust; Capt J G Wells RN, the Royal Naval Museum at Portsmouth, Capt Ray Parsons RN Director and Colin White Deputy Director; the Naval Historical Branch, David Brown; HMS Belfast Trust, Ron Fisher; HMS Cavalier Trust, the Submarine Museum at Gosport, Cdr Richard Compton-Hall RN; HMS Dolphin, Cdr Alastair Johnstone RN; Royal Marines Museum, Lt Col Keith Wilkins RM Director; Dr Richard Luckett Pepys Librarian Magdalene College Cambridge; the British Museum, Susan Youngs; the Victoria and Albert Museum; Sothebys; and John Tucker of *Navy News*.

Complementing the artists is the equally skilled work of the camera. The distinctive compositions of the noted aviation photographer Richard Wilson, much of it going back over the years obtained from RNAS Museum Yeovilton, depict the exploits of the Fleet Air Arm.

The life of the Royal Navy today, its ships and personnel, are portrayed in official Admiralty photography by the Director of Public Relations (Navy) Rear Admiral (then Captain) Guy Liardet and of special note are the efforts of the following: CPO (PHOT) Bob Stanyard, CPOs (PHOT) Charlie Gerbex, Jack Dewis, Chris McDermott, Ches Beech, Roger Ryan and Sgt Peter Williams RM, Sgt John Upsall RAF, WO (PHOT) Steve Dargan; also Lt Cdr R A Safe RN Fleet POs (PHOT) Photographic Unit Portsmouth, Capt Rob Need RM and Mike Reed for Royal Navy Chaplains.

Every picture may tell a story, but the scene has first to be set by the caption writer and for this and the extensive research involved we are indebted to Ben Sacks Ministry of Defence (Navy), assisted by Lt Cdr Stuart Bryden RN and Stuart Talbot-Longley Central Office of Information.

Between the assembly of all this material, through the efforts and dedication of so many individuals and organisations, and the finished volume in your hands, about we sincerely hope, to be crowned with your approval, lies the definitive task of editing and layout and we feel deeply grateful to Avril Evans of Seagull S.A. for the job she has done here and her never failing courtesy and patience in dealing with all involved in this production.

Finally, there is a heartfelt thank you to all those who have contributed to a greater or lesser degree and whom it is not possible to identify by name; not the least being the staff of this Fund, who have cheerfully borne the extra workload involved — only too well aware of what a glorious story it is to be told to the benefit of so worthwhile a cause.

Captain Keith Sutherland RN
General Secretary
King George's Fund for Sailors

Lieutenant Commander Maurice A Board RN
Appeals Director
King George's Fund for Sailors

The Royal Navy — 1000 Years of Peace and War

Contents

ROYAL NAVY — 1000 YEARS OF PEACE & WAR

897 — King Alfred's ship, designed for war at sea: note break in rows of oarports by a central deck.

1340 — A 14th Century NEF with solid castles. This type of ship was suitable without alteration for warlike or peaceful purposes.

Harold's ship — it was sailing between English ports when it was blown off course and took refuge in a Normandy harbour. He was seized by William who made his release conditional on his renunciation of his rights to the English throne. When Harold subsequently failed to honour this undertaking, William invaded England in 1066.

The English fleet on its way to meet the French at Sluys in Flanders, where Edward III completely defeated the French in 1340.

More than 1,000 years ago, the victory of an Anglo-Saxon King's Army gave birth to the concept of a King's Navy. The Battle of Uffington, its site in the Berkshire hills still marked by the great white horse carved in the chalk, saw not only the defeat of the invading Vikings by Alfred but also the realisation by the great Saxon King that the best means of defence lay in attack — and attack using the natural strength of his island Kingdom, the sea. Alfred copied the Viking longships to meet his ferocious enemies before they landed.

Comparative peace resulted from the development of three strategically placed fleets by succeeding monarchs and Edward the Confessor actually organised the provision of the now larger English roundships (from the shape of their bows) on a "contractual" basis by the creation of the Cinque Ports of Hastings, Romney, Sandwich, Dover, Hythe, Winchelsea and Rye, who in exchange for privileges undertook the provision of vessels for their area at certain times of the year. Otherwise they were engaged in their role as traders, including those bringing in wine in 'tuns', whence the measure of a ship's capacity (tonnage) derived. It was this summertime schedule in 1066 that probably cost Harold his Kingdom: his Norman foe waiting till the Saxon crews had laid up and were helping to get the harvest in.

The Conqueror applied his organisational zeal to the fledgling 'navy' (from the French navire for ship) too and Henry I and II also made their contributions. Portsmouth first became naval at this time and vessels increased in size and sophistication. Apart from the raised 'castles' in bow and stern, 'tops' (little galleries for archers) were added to masts; and the first naval artillery, in the form of 'engines' to catapult stones and burning pitch, started out on the long road to today's missiles.

Richard the Lionheart's Crusades, like the third in 1189, saw the

1189 — Richard I embarked at Dover in December 1189 for the Third Crusade to the Holy Land.

A Crusaders' ship with castles at each end. Most ships of this period steered by means of the side oars. It was not till the mid-13th Century that the side oar was removed to the sternpost as a rudder.

beginning of the English Navy's association with the Mediterranean and, with its transport of all the accoutrements of war including horses, was the first expeditionary force — the latest sailing South in 1982. King John's constitutional role overshadows his nautical one, but he appointed William de Wrotham 'Admiral' of the Fleet (though that rank from the Arabic 'Amir al Bahr' did not come in till much later) styled "Keeper of the King's Ships"; and he also achieved the greatest English success at sea to date, in Damme Harbour, after which he took the title "Governor of the Seas" and started the practice of requiring foreign ships to salute the English flag in the Channel, which was to be the spark for many a later conflict. After intermittent skirmishing with the French, such as the Battle of Dover in 1217, Edward III's claim to that throne too started the Hundred Years War. Though Southampton was burnt, the French fleet was routed on 24th June 1340 off the Flemish port of Sluys.

In 1346 the first great English army crossed the Channel in 700 ships to the Battle of Crecy, while the French fleet was besieged in Calais. In 1350 the Spanish were defeated off Winchelsea by a Fleet led by the King in person; who had also founded the "Court of the Admiralty" about this time, with administrative and judicial powers.

The first gunpowder manufactured in England in 1418 heralded a whole new era for all warfare but the real development of English seapower and its rising international ascendancy was to start with Henry VII and VIII, with the age of the great voyages of discovery, with all their promise of wealth from overseas to be won — and protected. The former's 'Regent' and 'Sovereign' built in 1488 were fourmasted technological masterpieces of their time, for which the first gravingdock was built at Portsmouth (on the site of the one used by *Victory* today).

And in Henry VIII's *Mary Rose* was another . . .

1399-1413 — The English "roundship" had a deeper draught, greater cargo carrying capacity and was a better sailer. She was an ideal ship for trade but needed considerable conversion before she became an effective man-o'-war.

*1066 — William the Conqueror's ship **Mora** which is not unlike the Viking ships known as "skeids" or "Drakkars".*

1217 — Battle of Dover, the French fleet was destroyed by the English.

FERRANTI plc

Mary Rose Trust.

*Visitors look into the massive oak timbers of the **Mary Rose** as if the hull were a giant cutaway model.*

*The **Mary Rose**. From a Tudor watercolour painted by Anthony Anthony.*

By permission of the Master and Fellows, Magdalene College, Cambridge.

Mary Rose Trust.

*Collection of domestic items recovered from the **Mary Rose** including a wooden tig, a pewter jug, wooden dishes, combs, a manicure set, a candlestick and various pewter and wooden items of cutlery.*

THE MARY ROSE

Mary Rose, King Henry VIII's favourite warship, now rests in a converted dry dock in Portsmouth Royal Naval Base, close to where she was first built in 1509-10. The *Mary Rose* was one of a pair of new ships built at Portsmouth, the other was named *Peter Pomegranate.* As a new ship, the *Mary Rose* fought well in a battle against the French in 1512, off Brest. A few months later, she out-sailed other ships of the King's fleet in Channel Trials and was described in a letter to the King from Sir Edward Howard, as "your good ship, the flower I trow of all ships that ever sailed". On a calm summer day in 1545, the *Mary Rose* set sail from Portsmouth to engage a French invasion fleet. As the King watched from Southsea Common, she suddenly heeled over and sank, barely a mile off shore. She took with her seven hundred men and the King is said to have heard their drowning cries as he witnessed the horrific event.

When divers discovered the wreck site, they found a time-capsule of Tudor life. Within the ship's hull lay the men who had fought and died on that warm July afternoon, four centuries ago, their weapons, their clothing and their possessions. In 1979, the Mary Rose Trust was formed to tackle the world's most ambitious underwater archaeological operation. HRH Prince Charles became its President and actively participated in the underwater explorations. In 1982, world-wide interest was captured when operations culminated with the raising of the hull itself, under the direction of the Trust's principal archaeologist Mrs Margaret Rule.

Excavations produced more than 14,000 objects, from the massive bronze cannons to intricately decorated pocket sun-dials, no bigger than a ten-pence piece. Of especial interest were the guns and their accessories, which gave an important insight into the naval ordnance of the times, and the long bows and arrows. Many of these artefacts are now on display in the Mary Rose Exhibition, housed in a Georgian timber boathouse, also in the Naval Base.

Inside the ship hall, the hull, now restored to the upright position, is sprayed continuously with chilled water and the atmosphere is controlled so as to keep the temperature low and the humidity high.

Archæologists are reconstructing the surviving starboard side of the ship, replacing timbers removed by divers when the *Mary Rose* lay on the sea bed. Visitors view the hull as though they were looking into some vast cut-away model.

Henry VIII's 700 ton timber ship was of revolutionary design — probably the first English warship to be purpose built to carry heavy guns between her decks. With the *Mary Rose* was born the wooden sailing warship — an ocean-going fighting machine that was to remain basically unaltered for three centuries.

National Maritime Museum, Greenwich.

SIR FRANCIS DRAKE AND THE LAUNCH OF THE FIRESHIPS

Sir Francis Drake, the great English Admiral was born near Tavistock in Devon in the year 1545. His father was a zealous Protestant and was forced to take refuge in Kent during the persecutions in the reign of Queen Mary, where he received a naval chaplaincy from Queen Elizabeth I. As a boy, Drake was educated by Sir John Hawkins, under whom he later served with gallant distinction.

On 13th December 1577, with a fleet of five small ships and 166 men he began the voyage to the Pacific through the Magellan Straits that was to earn him fame. He completed the voyage round the world, the first to be achieved by an Englishman, in two years and ten months. On his return, Queen Elizabeth I hesitated to recognise his achievements for fear of further alienating Spain, but she finally decided to honour him with a knighthood.

In 1585 he again went to sea, England by then being at war with Spain, and taking a fleet to the West Indies, captured several towns. It was in 1587 that he carried out one of his most famous exploits. He sailed for Lisbon with a fleet of thirty ships and there received intelligence of a great Spanish fleet being assembled in the Bay of Cadiz, as part of the Armada. With great courage he entered the port on 19th April and by a skilful use of fireships, succeeded in burning upwards of 10,000 tons of Spanish shipping, a feat which he later jocularly called "singeing the King of Spain's beard".

In 1588, when the Spanish Armada was approaching England, Sir Francis Drake was appointed Vice-Admiral under Lord Howard.

J.C. BAMFORD EXCAVATORS LTD

THE BATTLE OF THE DOWNS

The painting by Nooms, on display at the National Maritime Museum, depicts this famous 17th Century sea battle.

Towards the end of the year 1639 a magnificent Spanish Armada, comprising seventy-seven vessels and manned by some 24,000 sailors and soldiers, under the command of Admiral Oquendo, sailed in September of that year, into the English Channel. Their orders were to drive the Dutch from the narrow seas between England and France and to land a large army at Dunkirk.

The Spaniards were attacked by a small fleet of Dutch ships commanded by Admiral Marten Tromp and the Spanish fleet sought shelter under cover of the English Downs, alongside a squadron of English ships. Admiral Tromp kept the Spanish under surveillance until he received substantial reinforcements and then on 21st October 1639, boldly attacked them as they lay at anchor in English waters. The Spanish Admiral Oquendo, together with seven of his ships, managed to escape under the cover of a thick fog, but all the rest of his fleet was destroyed.

The crushing defeat of the Spanish assured command of the seas to the Dutch for the remainder of the war. The naval power of Spain never, in fact, recovered from the blow.

Old Admiralty Building as seen from Whitehall today.

DPR (N) M.o.D.

Samuel Pepys, Clerk of Acts 1662.

G. Kneller, National Maritime Museum, Greenwich.

THE ADMIRALTY BOARD ROOM

This famous room is housed in the Old Admiralty Building in Whitehall, which was designed by Thomas Ripley and erected between 1723 and 1725. Until the Admiralty House was completed in 1788, the First Sea Lord and other Lords of the Admiralty actually lived in the Admiralty Building, the Board Room being used as their office and sometimes as their dining-room.

The Admiralty Board Room is naturally steeped in Naval History. It has the distinction of having remained relatively unchanged as the control point of the Royal Navy for almost 250 years. It is used for meetings of the present Admiralty Board and many famous politicians and great sailors have worked or conferred there during its history.

In a wooden frame can be seen the original vellum appointing Samuel Pepys as 'Clerk of the Acts' in 1662. This was a relatively minor appointment with the Navy Board, but it started Pepys on his well known task of re-organising the Fleet in its systems of building ships, supplying stores and paying the seamen. Through his work he succeeded in eliminating many of the corrupt practices that had hitherto been employed and he established systems of administration that form the basis for those in use today. Pepys died in 1703, some 22 years before the Admiralty Building was completed. Also to be found in the Room is Lord St. Vincent's personal copy of "Regulations and Instructions relating to Her Majesty's Service at Sea", which he wrote, governing the conduct of the Fleet, when he became First Sea Lord at the start of the 19th Century.

Immediately over the fireplace and still in perfect working order, is the wind dial, which came from the earlier Admiralty Building and dates from 1708. It is actuated by a metal vane on the roof. Also on the roof was a large wooden semaphore by which urgent messages were relayed. This was done by teams of signalmen at prominent points, such as church towers en route. Some churches today still fly the White Ensign to commemorate this role. It is recorded that on one occasion, a message from the Board Room reached Portsmouth in twelve minutes by this method. The skyline above the Admiralty Building is still noted today for its array of radio aerials.

The seascape painting above the door was painted by Willem Van de Velde the Younger and the portrait of Nelson was painted by Cuzzardi, after the Battle of the Nile. The clock by the door, tells both the date and time and has stood in the Room since 1725.

The casket in the centre of the Board Room contains the flag of the Lord High Admiral which flew over the building before the Defence re-organisation in 1964. It is now only flown when Her Majesty The Queen, the present Lord High Admiral, is in the building.

Standing in this impressive room, it is easy to imagine the presence of all of those famous people who have shared in its history.

Old print of the Admiralty Board Room —   *— and today.*

DELTA GROUP plc   **CHARLES LETTS & CO LTD**   JOHNSON WAX

THE BURNING OF THE "ROYAL JAMES" AT THE BATTLE OF SOLE BAY, 28th MAY, 1672

The famous oil painting by the studio of Willem Van de Velde the Younger (1633-1707), a well known Dutch painter of sea pieces, is on display at the National Maritime Museum at Greenwich.

It depicts the burning of the *"Royal James"*, one of the English flagships at the Battle of Sole Bay on 28th May, 1672. This was the first naval engagement of the Third of the Dutch Wars during the second half of the 17th Century.

The Anglo-French allied fleet numbering some 100 ships joined forces at Portsmouth and set sail for the North Sea, but did not immediately take the offensive against the Dutch. The English ships were ill supplied and were compelled to anchor at Sole Bay, just to the north of Southwold on the Suffolk coast, in order to obtain water and provisions. The Dutch, under command of Admiral de Ruyter, discovered the Anglo-French fleet at anchor and fell upon them in a N.W. wind.

The Allied fleet went hurriedly into action, with the English Blue Squadron in the van, instead of its proper station at the rear. Thus the Allies were at once divided into two widely separated bodies and the Dutch admiral was able to concentrate nearly his whole force against the English ships. The flagship of the Duke of York *"Prince"* (100 guns) was so shattered that he was forced to leave her and go to the *"St. Michael"*. The *"Royal James"* (100 guns), the flagship of his second-in-command the Earl of Sandwich, fought gallantly for two hours and sank two fireships sent against her. However, a third grappled her successfully and she was set alight and destroyed with enormous loss of life. The Earl himself perished. His body was picked up three days later, so disfigured that it was only recognisable by the star on his coat.

The ships at the head of the English line at last tacked to support the centre and in the evening Admiral de Ruyter drew off his forces.

MARK TYZACK & SONS LTD   CHAMPION SPARKING PLUG CO LTD   IBM UNITED KINGDOM LTD   13

THE 'KINGFISHER' ENGAGING BARBARY PIRATES — 22 MAY 1681

In the Mediterranean, the seizure and plunder of ships by corsairs, or pirates as they became more commonly known, had been customary from time immemorial.

To the inhabitants of Algiers, Tunis and Tripoli, known then as the Barbary States, piracy was an old trade and the threat of capture and enslavement by the Barbary Corsairs was an ever-present danger to any ships sailing in those waters.

The situation worsened at the beginning of the 17th Century, when peace was made between England and Spain and The Netherlands and Spain. Privateering in the Caribbean was no longer permissible, so many experienced seamen were anxious to make their fortune in the old way by sailing the Mediterranean. They brought with them a type of square-rigged sailing vessel, hitherto unknown in the area — the galleon. These galleons were known often to be carrying great treasures among their cargoes. As the prosperity of the Western Mediterranean increased, so did the piracy of the Barbary Corsairs.

The Royal Navy's role of protecting British interests on the high seas was as important then as it is today and British Naval vessels maintained a permanent presence in this dangerous area of the Mediterranean at that time, often re-inforced by Dutch ships.

It was during one such patrol on 22nd May 1681 that the *Kingfisher,* a ship of 46 guns under the command of Captain Morgan Kempthorne, found herself off the coast of Sardinia. She was attacked by eight Algerian Barbary men-of-war, which immediately closed with her in rapid succession and at close range. The Corsair ships fired 'stink pots' as grenades, as well as guns. 'Stink pots' were a form of projectile which, upon breaking, produced a sudden burst of flame and thick, suffocating, sulpherous fumes.

The Barbary Admiral attempted to board *Kingfisher* and Captain Kempthorne was killed by a bullet in the head. Lieutenant Ralph Wrenn took command and the fight continued for over twelve hours, until the Algerian Corsairs broke off the action.

The *Kingfisher* was twice set on fire and suffered casualties of 8 killed and 38 wounded. Captain Morgan Kempthorne was buried in a fine tomb at Leghorn in Northern Italy.

All the drama of this early British naval action is captured in the painting by the Dutch artist, Willem van de Velde the Younger, which is on display at the National Maritime Museum at Greenwich.

W. Van de Velde the Younger, National Maritime Museum, Greenwich.

A. Storck, National Maritime Museum, Greenwich.

THE BATTLE OF THE TEXEL

This painting by Abraham Storck also shows the Battle of the Texel between an Anglo-French fleet commanded by Prince Rupert and the Dutch commanded by Admiral de Ruyter. Again, it shows the famous duel between Sir Edward Spragge, Admiral of the Blue Squadron, and Cornelius Tromp in the *Gouden Leeuw.* Both admirals were forced to shift their flags to other ships, and Spragge was shifting his for a second time when his boat was hit and he was drowned. No ship was taken by either side, and only an English yacht was sunk, but by keeping his fleet in being de Ruyter prevented the seaborne invasion that had been planned.

COOPERS & LYBRAND and COOPERS & LYBRAND ASSOCIATES

**CAPTAIN COOK — A CAUTIOUS LANDING, TANA,
NEW HEBRIDES — 1774**

Captain James Cook (1728-1779) the famous English naval Captain and explorer, was born at Marton, North Yorkshire on 28th October 1728.

He was apprenticed to Messrs Walker, Shipowners, of Whitby and in 1755, he joined the Royal Navy. After four years, he was appointed master of the sloop *Solebay* in which he was employed in the surveying of the St Lawrence River. In 1762 he was present at the recapture of Newfoundland and was appointed marine surveyor of the coastlines of Newfoundland and Labrador, making his name as a mathematician and astronomer.

In 1768, Cook was appointed to conduct an expedition on behalf of the Royal Society. He set sail in *Endeavour* (370 tons), together with several scientists. On 13th April 1769, he reached Tahiti and then sailed back to the South Pacific. He explored the Society Islands and then reached New Zealand, where he circumnavigated the coasts and charted them for the first time. He especially observed the channel separating North and South Islands, to which he gave his name, 'Cook Strait'. He then took passage to Australia, where he surveyed the entire east coast, naming New South Wales (because it resembled Glamorgan) and Botany Bay. These areas he took possession of for Great Britain.

He arrived back in England by way of the Cape of Good Hope in June 1770 and was made a Commander. Cook was soon to command another expedition "to determine once and for all the question of the supposed great southern continent". He sailed from Plymouth on 13 July 1772, with the *Resolution* (462 tons) and the *Adventure* (330 tons) and 193 men. The expedition again touched at the Cape of Good Hope and then sailed south-eastward, passing and re-passing into the Antarctic Circle and again reaching New Zealand. From here he resumed his search for the continent, sailing to Easter Island, Tonga, Tahiti and the New Hebrides. Next followed the discoveries of New Caledonia, Norfolk Island and the Isle of Pines. Eventually he succeeded in reaching Cape Horn, re-discovering South Georgia and discovering Sandwich Island, before visiting the Cape of Good Hope, St Helena and the Ascension Islands and the Azores. The voyage covered nearly three times the distance round the equator and lasted more than 1,000 days. In all this time and distance, Cook lost only one man and succeeded in mastering the scourge of scurvy, before returning to Plymouth on 25th July 1775. Cook's third and final voyage was to resolve the question of the North-West Passage. He volunteered for this task but was ordered to first sail into the Pacific in order to find a passage into the Atlantic. Sailing from Plymouth on 12th July 1776, he went first to the

Cape of Good Hope and then on to Tasmania, New Zealand, Tonga and the Society Islands, making several new discoveries on his way. From Tahiti he moved north, re-discovering the Sandwich Islands, first seen in 1555. He then surveyed the American west coast as far north as the Bering Strait and beyond, before making his way back to Hawaii. It was here that he met his death on 14th February 1779. During the night of 13th February one of *Discovery's* boats had been stolen by natives. In an endeavour to recover it, Captain Cook landed with a party of Marines. In the ensuing scuffle, Cook was overpowered by a crowd of natives. He was a remarkable man, who won the affection of those who served under him and distinguished honours were paid to the memory of this most intrepid explorer, who secured for Great Britain a large stake in Australasia.

Painting by William Hodges, who embarked with Captain Cook during his second voyage of discovery. It shows Cook landing cautiously at Tana in the New Hebrides, on 6th August 1774. During a previous landing, Cook had been surprised by the natives. Before landing in Tana, he ordered musket shots to be fired over the heads of the natives on shore, while **Resolution** *herself fired four-pounder shot. This had the desired effect and the natives of Tana received Cook in a friendly manner.*

GORDON'S GIN
(Established 1769)

THE BATTLE OF THE SAINTS — 12th APRIL 1782

'The Saints' are small rocky islets in the channel between the islands of Dominica and Guadaloupe, in the West Indies. The great sea battle fought among them off the Dominican coast on 12th April 1782, is among the most important in naval history and was undoubtedly the most considerable sea battle fought during the American War of Independence. It also saved Jamaica from a formidable attack.

The French commander, the Comte de Grasse, with 43 ships of the line was at Fort Royal in Martinique. His plan was to join with a Spanish force from Cuba and invade Jamaica. The British fleet, comprising 36 ships of the line commanded by Rodney was anchored at St. Lucia. On 8th April, the British sighted the French and Rodney immediately sailed in pursuit. On 9th April, eight ships of the British van were attacked by fifteen of the French, but de Grasse did not press the attack home as his ships were widely scattered. On 12th April, de Grasse recalled all his vessels and bore down towards the British. For two hours the two fleets, in line of battle, passed each other, the French steering south and the British north.

The fighting instructions, then in force, had not changed substantially for a hundred years. Battles were fought by opposing fleets sailing in line ahead on parallel courses. However, the variable winds blowing off the Dominican coast produced confusion on both sides and a great gap opened up in the French line. At first Rodney hesitated to part from the traditional order of battle, but after a few moments, he decided to steer his flagship *Formidable* through the opening, followed by six of his ships. This move forced many of the French ships to close action and the French were broken into three groups and completely disordered.

The Comte de Grasse, in his flagship *Ville de Paris* with five other vessels became isolated from his main force and after a gallant resistance were taken.

It was a general belief that many more French ships would have been captured if Rodney had pursued them more vigorously, but he was content with his efforts. Even Nelson wrote of the battle that it was "the greatest victory, if it had been followed up, that our country ever saw".

SAMUEL, FIRST VISCOUNT HOOD (1724-1816)

Samuel Hood, son of the vicar of Butleigh in Somerset, was born on 12th December 1724 and he entered the Navy on 6th May 1741. He served part of his time as a midshipman with Rodney in the *Ludlow* and became a Lieutenant in 1746. He captured French privateers in 1757 and captured the *Bellona* off Finisterre in 1759. During the war, his services were solely in the Channel and he was engaged, under Rodney in 1759 in destroying the vessels collected together by the French to serve as transports in the proposed invasion of England. In 1778 he became, somewhat unusually, commissioner of the dockyards at Portsmouth and governor of the Naval Academy, posts generally given to officers who were retiring from the sea. In 1780, when the King visited Portsmouth, he was made a baronet. On 26th September 1780, Hood was promoted rear-admiral and sent out to the West Indies to act as second-on-command to Rodney, to whom he was personally known. During Rodney's absence in England on sick leave, Hood was for a time in independent command and in the presence of a superior French force fought a well judged action with the French admiral the Comte de Grasse at Frigate Bay, St. Kitts in January 1782. When Rodney returned with reinforcements, the famous Battle of the Saints was fought, in which Hood played a brilliant part, personally capturing de Grasse's flagship the *Ville de Paris*.

Hood was made Vice-Admiral in 1787 and as a commander in the Mediterranean he occupied Toulon for six months in 1793 and captured Corsica in 1794. He was made a full Admiral in the same year, when he was recalled to England for political reasons and created Viscount Hood.

REAR ADMIRAL SIR SAMUEL HOOD'S ACTION — 29th MARCH 1781

On 29th March 1781, a squadron of British ships under the command of Rear Admiral Sir Samuel Hood, met up with a convoy of French ships commanded by the Comte de Grasse, the new French commander in the West Indies. Hood, who was British commander during Rodney's absence in England, was a long distance to lee of the French force and was, therefore, unable to close. As a result of these circumstances, no conclusive action took place.

Battle of the Saints, 1782.

ST. KITTS — 25th JANUARY 1782

On 25th January 1782, an action took place between Rear Admiral Sir Samuel Hood and the Comte de Grasse off the British held island of St. Kitts in the West Indies. Hood managed to lure de Grasse from off his anchorage off St. Kitts and then, by a skilful manoeuvre was able to anchor in his place. The battle that followed was the result of Comte de Grasse's unsuccessful efforts to move him from his anchorage.

PETROFINA (UK) LTD

THE GLORIOUS 1st JUNE 1794

This battle was the first great naval battle of the Wars of the French Revolution. It lasted for five days and culminated in victory for Lord Howe and one of the greatest successes in British Naval history. The battle was brought about by the need of the French revolutionaries to import large supplies of grain from North America and Britain's determination to prevent them. On 16th May 1794, the French fleet sailed from Brest to provide cover for the grain convoy. In spite of exceptionally foul weather,

Lord Howe brought the French fleet to action some 300 miles to the west of Brest and defeated their efforts to escape. His tactics were to close the enemy fleet, under the command of Villaret-Joyeuse, to break through the enemy line at all points and to engage from the leeward position. After four days of manoeuvring, the British fleet succeeded in their plan and broke through the enemy lines. As a result, a quarter of the French fleet was destroyed although the grain convoy still managed to reach France.

However, following the French defeat, there were no further great engagements at sea for the next two years.

In this painting, Lord Howe's flagship, the *Queen Charlotte* is trying to close with the *Montagne,* flagship of Admiral Villaret-Joyeuse. Unfortunately, just as she was coming up on the *Montagne's* starboard quarter, her fore-topmast was shot away and she fell back. Also shown are the *Valiant Orion,* the *Ramillies* and the *Majestic.*

THE BATTLE OF THE NILE — 1st AUGUST 1798

On 1st August 1798, Rear Admiral Sir Horatio Nelson (as he then was), commanding a force of fifteen ships of the line, including his flagship, *Vanguard,* successfully attacked a fleet of thirteen French ships in Aboukir Bay, some 15 miles north-east of Alexandria. This historic sea battle was a supreme example of Nelson's courage and audaciousness as a naval leader.

Early in the May of 1798, Napoleon and his army, together with the French Admiral Brueys in 13 ships of the line, including *L'Orient* (120 guns) and several frigates, had managed to escape the British blockade and reach Malta. On 10th June, they set sail with the intention of capturing Egypt and disrupting British trade with India.

Meanwhile, Nelson, with a slightly smaller force, was in Naples, searching for the French. Nelson also set sail for Egypt on 17th June and at one time, the two fleets had barely 60 miles of sea between them, but neither was aware of the other's presence. On the night of 22nd June, the two fleets actually crossed tracks. On 29th June, Nelson reached Alexandria, but the French were not there, so Nelson set course for Sicily. On 1st July, the French landed at Alexandria and occupied the anchorage and the town. The Battle of the Pyramids was won by Napoleon on 21st July and Bonaparte became master of Egypt. Nelson, meanwhile, was still searching for the French and on 19th July 1798 had reached Syracuse, where he obtained water and provisions and the firm news that the French had gone to Egypt.

On 24th July, Nelson again sailed south-eastwards and on 1st August was once more off to Alexandria. He had knowledge of the location of the French fleet and despite their strong position and the lateness of the hour, he attacked immediately. The French were totally unprepared for an attack from the landward side and several British ships took considerable risk, by sailing inside the French line in very shallow water. The small boats, prominent in the painting, show how much the French were caught unawares, for as soon as Nelson's Fleet arrived there was a great scramble to get the crews back on board their rightful ships, to engage the British.

Robert Taylor's painting shows the battle at approximately 1800, after the French had been solidly engaged. At 2130 the French flagship, *L'Orient* was seen to be on fire and at 2200 she blew up, with the loss of Admiral Brueys and Commodore Casabiana and his son. It was this incident which is described in the famous lines "the boy stood on the burning deck". The violent explosion of *L'Orient* caused a brief lull in the battle, but it soon recommenced, ending at around midnight.

Only the French ships *"Guillaime Tell"* and *"Genereux"*, together with two frigates, succeeded in escaping from the roadstead at Aboukir. The destruction of the French Fleet isolated Napoleon in Egypt and had a profound political influence in Europe. The degree of French losses was never fully ascertained, but they were known to be massive. British losses amounted to 218 killed and 678 wounded. Nelson was disabled by a head wound.

The result of this famous victory was that Nelson regained control of the Mediterranean, thwarting Napoleon's plans to capture Egypt and invade India.

BPB INDUSTRIES PLC

LORD NELSON WITH LADY HAMILTON AND HORATIA

Reproduced by kind permission Royal Navy Museum, Portsmouth.

No book relating to the history of the Royal Navy would be complete without due reference to England's greatest naval hero. Horatio Nelson was born on 29th September 1758 at the village of Burnham Thorpe in Norfolk. He was the son of a Norfolk clergyman, attended High School in Norwich and then went to sea with his uncle, Captain Maurice Suckling, in the *Raisonable* a ship of 64 guns.

As a Naval Officer he always took the offensive, exposing his ship to enemy fire and achieving tremendous victories, often against severe odds. At the Battle of Cape St. Vincent in 1797, he carried out an audacious manoeuvre against the Spanish line and offered himself to their attack.

This move led to their defeat. At the Battle of the Nile in 1798, against the French, he managed to all but annihilate the enemy squadron. In 1801, at the Battle of Copenhagen, the famous incident occurred when he raised his telescope to his blind eye and pretended that he had not seen the signal to withdraw. His example was an inspiration to both the officers and men under his command. It was at the Battle of Trafalgar in 1805 that he set the seal on his fame with the famous signal "England expects that every man this day will do his duty". At Trafalgar, he achieved a brilliant victory, unfortunately at the cost of his life.

Nelson lived with Emma, Lady Hamilton, for seven years and she bore

him a daughter, Horatia, whom they both adored. For a while, their romance caused a great scandal in London society and on one occasion, the King even turned his back on Nelson at a reception. His love of Emma made Nelson feel complete. From the moment he met her, he was a man of two loves; his love of honour, duty, the navy and glory and the men he served with and his love of Emma.

The immortal memory of Nelson is still revered, especially in the Navy. He is remembered not only because he was a great admiral and tactician and a great hero, but also because he was an exceptionally kind and loveable man.

This picture depicts the battle at just about 13.00 hours, on October 21st, 1805.

THE BATTLE OF TRAFALGAR

The Battle of Trafalgar, the most decisive naval action of the French Revolutionary Wars and of British History, took place on 21st October 1805. Its outcome enabled Britain to dominate control of the seas and finally dashed any hopes that Napoleon had of invading England.

The British Fleet, commanded by Vice-Admiral Lord Nelson, attacked the combined French and Spanish Fleet of 33 ships of the line. Abandoning the standard naval tactics of sailing parallel to the enemy line, Nelson's bold and simple plan was to attack Admiral Villeneuve's fleet at right-angles and break the enemy line in two places.

Thus, the British Fleet attacked in two columns. Nelson led the port column in HMS *Victory* and Collingwood, his second-in-command, the starboard column in HMS *Royal Sovereign*. The action was carried out exactly as planned, despite the light wind and sea currents, which demanded the highest qualities of seamanship. The fighting lasted for four hours and twenty enemy ships were taken prize, or lowered their colours. Nelson's flagship became heavily engaged during the battle and was raked by enemy fire, taking much punishment, including damage to her rigging and mizzen mast. The French ship, *Redoubtable* was locked in battle alongside *Victory* and a French sniper, aloft in the fighting-top of this ship, fired the fatal shot which struck Nelson down. Nelson died just after hearing the news of his overwhelming victory and Collingwood assumed command of the British Fleet.

Nelson's tactics had been sound and no British ship struck her colours or was boarded, while few of the enemy fleet escaped capture or destruction. However, in the British Fleet, the reported losses were 1690 killed and wounded and of these 1452 belonged to 14 out of the 27 ships of the line engaged.

*Vice-Admiral Nelson's Flagship **Victory** had just broken through the lines of the French and Spanish Fleet. A broadside from her port cannons has crippled Admiral Villeneuve's French Flagship, the **Bucentaure**, and she is firing another broadside at the **Santisima Trinidad**. Just astern and to starboard the **Temeraire** manoeuvres to trap the **Redoubtable** (on the extreme left of the painting).*

OCEAN TRANSPORT & TRADING PLC (P. H. HOLT TRUST)

Clarkson Stanfield, United Services Club.

The barge that carried Nelson's body to St. Paul's: this can be seen at the Victory Museum at Portsmouth.

Victory Museum, Portsmouth.

AFTER TRAFALGAR — HMS 'VICTORY' RETURNS TO GIBRALTAR

The fierce storm which followed the Battle of Trafalgar gave the French an opportunity to retake some of their ships, which had been seized as prizes. Many other ships, from both sides, were swept into the bay between Trafalgar and Cadiz and were lost.

Only four ships were taken into Gibraltar by the British fleet, three of these were French and one Spanish. Only eleven of the allied fleet succeeded in finding safety in Cadiz. A fragment of the French Squadron, under Admiral Rosily, remained there until he was forced to surrender to the Spaniards in 1808, on the outbreak of the Peninsular War.

The artist Clarkson Stanfield R.A. (1793-1867) painted three well-known pictures connected with the Battle of Trafalgar. The painting shown depicts HMS *Victory,* with the body of Nelson on board and her ensigns flying at half mast, being towed into Gibraltar on 28th October 1805, seven days after the battle and the fierce storm that followed.

The artist has recorded the poignant moment when HMS *Victory* returned to join the fleet after the great British triumph and the tragic death of Nelson. The painting was very well received as a great dramatic composition and moved many of those who saw it to write poetic verses.

GIBRALTAR SHIPREPAIR LTD.

THE *BELLEROPHON* AT PLYMOUTH WITH NAPOLEON ON BOARD

After Napoleon's defeat at the Battle of Waterloo in June 1815, the Congress of Vienna banished him from Europe. Forced to abdicate, Napoleon attempted to flee to the United States of America, but was prevented from leaving France by a blockade of the ports. He then appealed to the British Government, who instructed him to board one of the blockading Royal Navy warships the *Bellerophon,* whose commanding officer was Captain F.L. Maitland. When the *Bellerophon* reached Plymouth in August 1815, Napoleon was transferred to the *Northumberland,* which set sail almost immediately for St. Helena. The exiled Napoleon arrived on this isolated island in the South Atlantic in October 1815. He died on St. Helena in 1821.

The painting of 'the *Bellerophon* at Plymouth with Napoleon on board' by J.J. Chalon has certainly captured the excitement of the occasion, with boats full of the local gentry all eager to get a look at Napoleon. Ironically, this was the closest that Napoleon ever got to the shores of England.

THE BATTLE OF NAVARINO

The Battle of Navarino was fought on 20th October 1827 and is sometimes described as the last great battle of the sailing navy, for steam propulsion was soon to take over. British ships, under the command of Vice-Admiral Sir Edward Codrington, had been sent to the Mediterranean to aid in the liberation of Greece from the oppressions of the Ottoman Empire, of which she then formed part. There had been a steadily growing revolt against the harsh rule of the Turks and the demands of the oppressed Greeks were backed by Britain, France and Russia, who jointly agreed to demand an armistice from the Turks as a forerunner to a full settlement of Greece's independence.

The Turkish government refused to accept the armistice and Sir Edward Codrington and his fleet, hearing that an Egyptian convoy was on its way from Alexandria to re-inforce the Turks, sailed to intercept it. On 12th September, he found the Egyptian ships at anchor with a Turkish squadron at Navarino. He kept his forces a little way off, thinking that the Turks would sign the armistice. On 19th September he noted a movement among the Turkish and Egyptian ships in the bay and informed the Ottoman Admiral, Tahir Pasha, that he had orders to prevent any hostile movement against the Greeks. The allied fleets now separated to replenish their stores, leaving frigates to watch Navarino.

From 3rd October to 5th October, Admiral Codrington was engaged in turning back the Egyptian and Turkish vessels. By general agreement, he was in overall command of the allied fleet and his forces comprised his flagship the *Asia* (84 guns) leading three British, four French and four Russian sail of the line, together with four British, one French and four Russian frigates and six British and French brigs and schooners. The Egyptians and Turks had three lines of battleships and fifteen large frigates, with many small craft, raising the total number of their assorted vessels to over 80.

On 17th October 1827, the allied admirals decided to enter Navarino Bay and anchor among the Egyptian and Turkish ships. On the 20th, Captain Fellowes, the officer commanding the British frigate *Dartmouth* (42 guns) saw a Turkish fireship close to windward and sent a boat with a demand that it be removed. The Turks fired on the boat, killing Lieutenant G. W. H. Fitzroy, who was carrying the message, and several of the boat's crew. The *Dartmouth* then opened defensive fire and the battle became general among the anchored ships, who were all closely engaged. The allied fleet achieved victory by their better gunnery and heavier broadsides. Threequarters of the Turkish and Egyptian vessels were sunk and there were heavy casualties on both sides.

The Battle of Navarino was one of the decisive battles of World history. It not only destroyed the efforts of the Turks to suppress the Greeks, but it also made a break in the traditional friendship between Great Britain and Turkey. Additionally, by the annihilation of the Ottoman navy, it precipitated the Russo-Turkish war of 1828-29.

National Maritime Museum, Greenwich.

BOMBARDMENT OF ALGIERS — PELLEW FREES SLAVES

For centuries the commerce of the European nations in the Mediterranean had suffered from the depredations of pirates based along the shores of North Africa. By the early 19th Century, Algiers had become notorious as the stronghold of these Barbary pirates and the scourge of the Mediterranean. On 27th August 1816, Sir Edward Pellew commanding a fleet of 25 English and Dutch warships, attacked this heavily fortified city. After nine hours of fierce fighting and bombardment, the large Barbary fleet was burned and the harbour fortifications including the arsenal, destroyed. Some 3,000 Christian slaves were released from captivity.

In the painting by George Chambers the Elder, the full extent of the destruction is vividly illustrated. Pellew's flagship, the *Queen Charlotte* can be seen in the centre of the painting near the mole, with the damaged *Impregnable* to the right. On the left, are the *Minden* and the *Superb,* the Dutch frigates and a glimpse of the *Albion.* On his return to England following the action, Sir Edward Pellew was created 1st Viscount Exmouth.

WATKINS-JOHNSON UK OPERATIONS

GEEST HOLDINGS LTD

CONSTANTINE HOLDINGS LTD

THE ROYAL HOSPITAL AT GREENWICH

    This painting of the Royal Hospital by Canaletto dates from about 1755 and the Venetian artist has graced the River Thames with the romance of his own waterways. At the centre, in the distance, can be seen the Queen's House, started by Inigo Jones in 1617, but only completed in the reign of Charles I. To the right is the King Charles House, built by Webb in 1666 and to the left is the Queen Anne Block, which was part of Wren's original design which was completed by his assistants Campbell and Ripley. The tower on the left stands above the Chapel and that on the right above the famous Painted Hall. The view is across the River from the Isle of Dogs where, traditionally, the king's hunting hounds were kennelled.

    The buildings as seen today are a Baroque masterpiece, designed by Sir Christopher Wren in 1695 as a Hospital for aged and infirm seamen of the Royal Navy. They were originally the site of a Royal Palace, the favourite resort of Tudor Monarchs and the birth place of Henry VIII, Mary and Elizabeth I. Under Cromwell, the palace went into decay and Charles II, on his restoration, aimed to replace it with a grand new palace in the Classical style. However, only the King's House was built. William and Mary preferred living at Hampton Court and donated the palace at Greenwich for use as a Naval Hospital, similar to the Army Hospital at Chelsea. One of their conditions was that the two existing Royal Houses with their views

of the River be preserved and Wren achieved this by altering the course of the River and incorporating the Houses in a magnificent symetrical design.

    The Greenwich Hospital held nearly 5,000 Pensioners until it closed in 1869. In 1873, the Admiralty took over the buildings for use as the Royal Naval College and it is now regarded as the Navy's University, providing advanced education in Defence Studies and Staff Work and in nuclear science and technology. The famous Painted Hall serves as a Banqueting Hall for the Crown, The Government and the Admiralty Board and the beauty of the Rococo style Chapel is a great attraction.

HENDERSON ADMINISTRATION LIMITED   BASS plc   WOOLWICH EQUITABLE BUILDING SOCIETY

HMS *WARRIOR* — BRITAIN'S FIRST IRON BATTLESHIP

In the early 19th century, the change from wood to iron for ship construction was gradually increasing, though not without opposition from supporters of "Hands off our wooden walls" to those who said "But iron won't float".

At a time of tension between Britain and France, the Admiralty ordered the construction of HMS *Warrior* to counter the French building programme of ironclads, led by the *Gloire*. Launched in December 1860 and completed the following year, *Warrior* emerged as the largest, fastest, best protected and most formidable warship in the world.

Whilst *Gloire* displaced 5700 tons and had an armoured wooden hull, *Warrior,* also a frigate, was built of wrought iron. Three times the size of *Victory* and displacing 9210 tons, she had a length of 400 feet. Her single gun deck, with a powerful broadside capability, was protected by a 4½ inch thick iron belt, backed by 18 inches of teak. She had a speed of more than 14 knots and was powered by twin cylinder horizontal engines. She also had a full outfit of masts and sails.

In 1863 she had a complement of 50 officers and 650 ratings. After she commissioned in 1861, her gunnery officer was the dynamic Lieutenant Jackie Fisher, later to become First Sea Lord. After three uneventful commissions, she was put into reserve. In 1904 she was re-named *Vernon III* and became part of the floating Torpedo School at Portsmouth. Subsequently in 1929, she was towed to Llannion Cove by Pembroke Dock in Milford Haven to become a floating jetty on which to berth oil tankers and ships needing fuel.

Warrior was rescued by the Maritime Trust in 1979 and was towed to Hartlepool to be re-constructed to her original condition by the *Warrior Preservation Trust* at the cost of £4m. The restoration has been carried out with uncommon skill by the Hartlepool local workforce, including many trainees from the Manpower Services Commission.

It is planned for the *Warrior* to be towed to Portsmouth in April 1987 for public display in a berth afloat provided by the Portsmouth City Council.

The next ship to bear the name *Warrior* was an armoured cruiser, which took part in the Battle of Jutland in 1916 and was so severely damaged that she had to be abandoned and sunk. During World War II, an aircraft carrier of 13,350 tons displacement bore the name until she was sold in 1958. HMS *Warrior* is also the name of one of the Royal Navy's "Stone Frigates", a shore establishment at Northwood, Middlesex, which wears the flag of the Commander-in-Chief Fleet.

DPR (N) M.o.D.

THE IMMORTAL *WARRIOR*

The definitive history of HMS *Warrior,* written by Captain John Wells and covering the concept, building, trials and career up to last stages of reconstruction, will be ready early in 1987. The publisher, Kenneth Mason of the Old Harbourmaster's, Emsworth, Hants, hopes to publish the book entitled "The Immortal *Warrior*" to coincide with the ship's arrival at Portsmouth. *Apply to publisher for further details.*

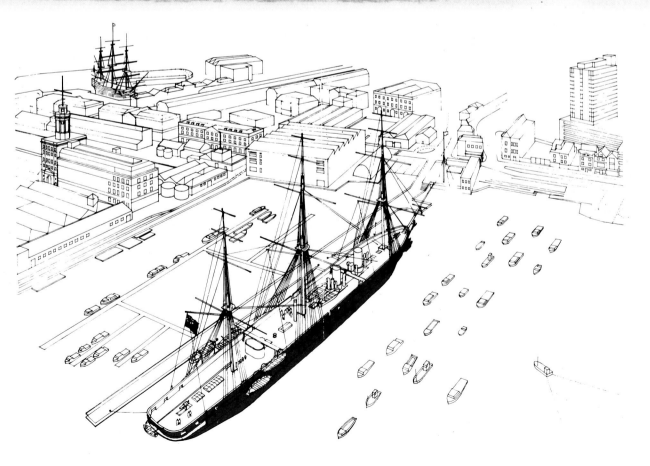

National Maritime Museum, Greenwich.

QUEEN VICTORIA'S DIAMOND JUBILEE

In Charles Dixon's painting of Queen Victoria's Diamond Jubilee Fleet Review at Spithead on 26th June 1897, can be seen the might of the Royal Navy, then the largest and most powerful navy in the world. On the right of the picture can also be seen the Royal Yacht *Victoria and Albert* flying the Royal Standard.

On board the Royal Yacht was the Prince of Wales (later Edward VII) representing the Queen, and a number of guests including the Empress Frederick of Germany whose standard was also hoisted, the Duke of Coburg and the Duke of York. On review were over 160 warships of the Royal Navy and a small number of foreign warships.

In the evening after the review, the Fleet was illuminated 'by means of thousands upon thousands of incandescent electric lamps', which 'were so arranged as completely to outline each vessel, with her masts, tops, bridges, and barbettes, or turrets'. The illumination of the Fleet proved even more popular than the review itself and large crowds lined the nearby beaches and the shores of the Solent to witness this grand spectacle.

 ABBEY NATIONAL BUILDING SOCIETY   FURNESS WITHY AGENCY LIMITED   NORCROS plc

BRITANNIA ROYAL NAVAL COLLEGE — DARTMOUTH

Plans for a permanent Royal Naval College, for the training of Naval Officers, overlooking the anchorage of the old 'Britannia' on the River Dart, were approved in 1900. Five years later, in 1905, the solid Edwardian buildings of stone and red brick were completed and became the heart of the College as it is today.

It was no mere chance that made Dartmouth the home of the Britannia Royal Naval College. The beautiful natural harbour on the South Devon coast and the River Dart itself are part of British Naval history. In the first Elizabethan era, Dartmouth ships sailed forth to fight the Spanish Armada and one of the first Spanish prizes was brought triumphantly home to the port. When first-class ships of the line became too large for the river anchorage, Dartmouth ceased to be a naval base, but it has always remained a busy port.

The Britannia Royal Naval College is essentially a practical place. The Royal Navy needs many new Officers every year and the Naval Officers produced by Dartmouth need to be totally involved in the modern world, whilst retaining the Royal Navy's cherished traditions. The training at Dartmouth has kept pace with technological change.

The 18th Century practice of sending a boy to sea with a Captain known personally to the boy's parents was replaced first by a Naval Academy at Portsmouth and then by training ships at Portsmouth, Portland and finally at Dartmouth. Since 1863, the training of Naval Officers has been based on the River Dart and until the present College was built, it actually took place in the fine old harbour hulk 'Britannia', a former sailing ship of the line.

When the Britannia Royal Naval College first opened, boys joined at the age of 13 and remained for four years before going to sea as Cadets. Three years later, they would return for a further course at the Naval College at Greenwich.

In the past, most entrants to Dartmouth came from boarding schools. Today they come from all parts of the educational spectrum and include some from foreign and Commonwealth navies.

If one had to choose a single word to describe Dartmouth it would be "activity", since Nelson's time, an expression of high praise in the Royal Navy.

Many famous Admirals began their naval careers at Dartmouth and a number of the sons of British and foreign Royal Families have taken advantage of the Dartmouth education. These have included Admiral of the Fleet the Earl Mountbatten, who was a Midshipman at the College when it was mobilised at the outbreak of World War I; His Majesty King George VI; Prince Philip Duke of Edinburgh; HRH Prince Charles Prince of Wales and his brother HRH Prince Andrew, who distinguished himself as a helicopter pilot during the Falklands Campaign.

Training at Dartmouth concentrates on three main areas — professional, character and leadership and academic. In recent years Dartmouth has broadened its intake to include WRNS Officers, Royal Marines, Chaplains, Instructor Officers, Special Duties Officers, Officers of the Medical Branches, QARNNS Nursing Officers and List 1 Royal Naval Reserve Officers. Staff and Lecturers are of the highest calibre in the Service and of a standard equal to the best Universities.

COI M.o.D.

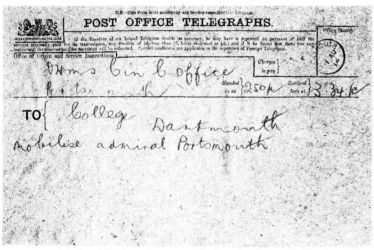

The original mobilisation telegram, received on the afternoon of 1st August 1914, is still preserved at Dartmouth.

*Until the beginning of this century, HMS **Britannia** and HMS **Hindustan**, former sailing ships of the line, were used as training ships for naval cadets.*

PILKINGTON BROTHERS PLC

FLEMING-WILLIAMS, I.W.M.

'RELEASE OF THE HAWK'

The painting by C. R. Fleming-Williams depicts a Sopwith 2F1 Camel rising from a lighter, towed behind a destroyer of Harwich Force during the last months of the First World War. The Camel has been launched to intercept a Zeppelin over the North Sea.

Lighters were originally used to transport large flying-boats across the North Sea to increase their radius of action over the Heligoland Bight area.

Towards the end of the war, lighters with take-off platforms were used to launch fighter aircraft and the first successful take-off was achieved by Lieutenant S. D. Culley in a Sopwith Camel on 31st July 1918. A few days later the same officer shot down a Zeppelin whilst operating from a lighter. This was the last Zeppelin of the war to be destroyed in air combat.

The main role of the Sopwith 2F1 Camel, which was specifically designed

as a shipboard fighter for the Royal Naval Air Service, was to intercept and destroy Zeppelins over the North Sea. In addition to being operated from towed lighters, Camels were also carried in warships, being flown off from platforms mounted above gun turrets and were operated from aircraft carriers.

THE ALEXANDRA TOWING COMPANY LIMITED

Charles Pears, I.W.M.

STEAM PINNACES AT HAWES PIER

Laying in the shadow of the Forth railway bridge, Naval steam pinnaces wait at Hawes Pier to embark officers and men for transportation to their ships anchored in the Firth of Forth. This picture was painted by Charles Pears, towards the end of the First World War.

In addition to serving as an anchorage for the Fleet, the Royal Naval Dockyard and base was also situated at nearby Rosyth. The rapid growth of the Imperial German Navy, before World War I, had been of great concern to the Admiralty and the need to concentrate both ships and men on the east coast of Scotland became a matter of great importance. The busy flow of traffic, constantly moving up and down the river and across the bridge, both by day and night, served to emphasise the importance of this crucial Naval Base.

Life at sea, in those days of coal-fired ships was hard work and one can imagine the feelings of relief and pleasure as the liberty boats discharged their passengers for a welcome run ashore. Likewise, the feelings of urgency and grim determination as the men waited to embark are apparent in the painting.

A RUN ASHORE

A good run ashore is always an enjoyable occasion. None the more so when the opportunity occurs on a visit to a foreign port. Here we see a group of naval ratings, dressed in their tropical white rig, making the most of such a visit.

The opportunity for foreign travel in the Navy is still a great attraction and though the chances are perhaps a little less frequent today, they still exist in no small measure and are an attractive consideration for anyone thinking of joining the Naval Service.

DPR (N) M.o.D.

Herbert Hillier, I.W.M.

THE DAWN OF ANZAC DAY — SUNDAY, 25th APRIL, 1915

With Turkey aligned with the Central Powers during the First World War, it was considered advisable for the Allies to control the narrow straits of the Dardanelles in order to have access to Constantinople (Istanbul) and the Black Sea, so that essential weapons and munitions could be supplied to Russia. An unsuccessful attempt was made early in 1915 to force the Dardanelles passage with warships, after which the Turkish Army reinforced the Gallipoli peninsula in strength. An amphibious landing was therefore planned.

On 25th April, 1915 the Australian and New Zealand Army Corps under Sir William Birdwood landed on the peninsula at a spot since known as Anzac Cove and at the same time other British forces landed further along the coast.

This striking painting by Herbert Hillier illustrates the preliminary bombardment at dawn of the Turkish positions on the peninsula by the Fleet prior to the landings. On the left of the painting, the battleship *Queen Elizabeth* is moving into position, while other warships have commenced firing. Although the 30,600 ton *Queen Elizabeth* was completed in 1915 and carried a main armament of eight 15 inch guns, the majority of the assembled Fleet were warships of the pre-*Dreadnought* era.

ANZ MERCHANT BANK LTD

Beatty on the bridge: Private collection
of Lieut.-Com. M. Board.

R. SMITH, I.W.M.

JUTLAND — HISTORY'S FINAL BATTLEFLEET ENGAGEMENT

The Battle of Jutland, the greatest naval engagement of the First World War, was fought between the Grand Fleet of Great Britain and the High Seas Fleet of Germany on 31st May 1916. Both Fleets were divided into two distinct units; the advanced forces of battlecruisers, battleships, cruisers and destroyers, commanded respectively on the two sides by Vice-Admiral Sir David Beatty and Vice-Admiral Franz von Hipper and the main fleets of battleships, cruisers and destroyers commanded by Admiral Sir John Jellicoe and Vice-Admiral Reinhard Scheer.

On 30th May, intelligence reports were received in the Admiralty indicating that the German High Seas Fleet was preparing to go to sea from their base at Wilhemshaven and the Grand Fleet was ordered to proceed to sea, to carry out a search in the eastern area of the North Sea in the hope of making contact with the enemy. That evening, the main fleet sailed from its bases at Scapa Flow and Invergordon and the battlecruiser force from Rosyth. Beatty's advance force was some sixty miles ahead of the main fleet. Early the following morning Hipper's force sailed from Wilhelmshaven and proceeded towards the Norwegian coast, followed by Scheer's mainforce some fifty miles astern. At this stage, neither side had definite knowledge that the other was at sea.

Early in the afternoon of 31st May, Beatty's force, having carried out a sweep off the Skagarrak, was about to turn north when HMS *Galatea,* one of his light cruiser screen, stopped to check a merchant ship and at the same time sighted a German cruiser, which also saw the *Galatea.* Both ships immediately transmitted "enemy in sight" signals. Beatty turned his force to the south and by the middle of the afternoon was in action with Hipper's ships. Beatty forced the action to the utmost and both sides suffered heavy damage. HMS *Indefatigable* and HMS *Queen Mary* were both sunk and when Scheer's main force arrived on the scene, Beatty was outnumbered. He altered course to the north towards Jellicoe's fast approaching battleships.

The two main fleets came into contact just after 1800, about eighty miles west of the coast of Jutland. Due to the lack of precise information, Jellicoe did not know the position of Scheer's force until the last moment. However, he decided to deploy his fleet into line of battle on the port wing, a tactical stroke, which not only placed his ships across the line of the German retreat to their base, but also crossed the "T" of their line of battle. From then until nightfall, in misty weather conditions, the ships were involved in a fierce battle, causing some heavy damage on both sides and HMS *Invincible* was sunk.

As the night closed in, both fleets steamed in 'Night Formation' to the south. Jellicoe did not consider that a night action was advisable and was confident that the battle would be won in the morning. For Scheer, it was essential that he got his now outnumbered and battered force, which was to the west of the Grand Fleet, back to their base, otherwise they were doomed to destruction in the morning. He therefore decided to cross astern of Jellicoe's ships and though meeting fierce opposition from the British cruisers and destroyers and losing his battleship *Pommern,* he finally reached the security of the German minefields in the Heligoland Bight. When dawn broke, the sea was empty and the British Grand Fleet turned northwards for its bases.

In the context of World War I, as a whole, the battle was a strategic victory for Great Britain, although the Grand Fleet lost more tonnage and sustained more casualties than the German High Seas Fleet. After Jutland, the German High Seas Fleet hardly ever put to sea again.

PLESSEY DEFENCE SYSTEMS LIMITED

A CORNER OF THE DOCKYARD, ROSYTH

Charles Pears, I.W.M.

Rosyth Dockyard under snow, sailors walk through the dockyard complex during the winter of 1918. On the left of the picture is the dockyard power station, while the battleship HMS *Canada* can be seen in the nearest dock.

With the growth of Britain as a maritime power, also came the requirement for dockyards in which to build and maintain the ships needed to protect our commercial and strategic interests. Portsmouth possessed a thriving dockyard by the end of the 15th Century and the first dry dock was built here in 1495. The next Royal Dockyards to be constructed were at Woolwich and Deptford, followed by Chatham in 1547. Royal Dockyards were also built at Sheerness and Devonport, originally known as Plymouth Dock and completed at the end of the 17th Century. At the beginning of the 19th Century, Pembroke was established as a shipbuilding yard and a century later in response to the growing naval might of Germany, Rosyth was hastily built and proved its worth during two world wars.

Today only Devonport, Rosyth and a slimmer-look Portsmouth survive as Royal Dockyards.

BABCOCK INTERNATIONAL plc

WRNS working in canvas shop, Essex.

FORBES: I.W.M.

WRNS: Formed 1917.

WOMEN'S ROYAL NAVAL SERVICE RATINGS
SAIL MAKING IN 1918

In November 1917, the Admiralty recommended the formation of a women's service, with the aim of releasing more men for active service at sea. Sir Eric Geddes, the then First Lord of the Admiralty, informed King George V, who gave the proposal his Royal approval.

It was originally intended that the ladies should be employed on mainly domestic and clerical duties. However, from the outset, they were never limited by the traditional ideas of 'women's work' and they performed all manner of menial and essential tasks.

The person appointed to set up the organisation of the Women's Royal Naval Service was Dame Katherine Furse, who had recently had experience of working with women in the Red Cross. She became the first Director WRNS from November 1917 until December 1919.

A new-entry training establishment for WRNS Ratings was established at Crystal Palace, under the Direction of Miss Vera Laughton (later to become Dame Vera Laughton Mathews, Director WRNS from April 1939 until November 1946). Its purpose was to give adequate instruction in the ways of the Royal Navy to the new recruits and professional job training for each girl joining the WRNS. A college for training WRNS Officers was

opened at nearby Ashurst and the first WRNS Officers entered service, at naval bases and stations, on 18 January 1918.

Many of the first WRNS were volunteers, from all walks of life, and the Service rapidly grew to a peak. In 1918, the WRNS' strength numbered 438 Officers and 5,054 Ratings. Very soon, they were not only cleaning, cooking and doing office work; they were also driving trucks and motor bikes, piloting small boats, cleaning boilers, making and mending sails, priming depth charges, working long hours as telegraphists and cypher clerks and generally turning their hands to a host of other vital tasks, previously done by the men.

The Royal Navy was full of praise for its gallant sisters in uniform. However, at the end of World War I, it was decided to demobilise all the WRNS and despite Dame Katherine Furse's enthusiastic attempts to preserve her Service, it was officially disbanded on 1st October 1919. Little did anyone then imagine that in less than twenty years, the WRNS would be re-formed to face an even more daunting and demanding wartime challenge.

Algernon Black, I.W.M.

BRITISH AIRSHIPS ESCORTING TRANSPORTS

A convoy of troop transports being escorted in home waters by Naval airships and warships during 1917/18.

The first British airship was constructed for the Admiralty in 1908. When No.1 Rigid Naval Airship, known unofficially as the 'Mayfly' was wrecked in 1911, Naval airship development was severely curtailed and no further orders were placed until two rigid and six non-rigid airships were authorised in July 1913. In November 1913, all airships operated by the British Army were handed over to the Naval Wing of the Royal Flying Corps, which became the Royal Naval Air Service in July 1914. Airships remained under the control of the Admiralty until December 1919.

From March 1915 onwards, small non-rigid airships were constructed for the RNAS and used for anti-submarine patrol, convoy escort and coastal reconnaisance duties. The development of these airships can be traced through the Sea Scout, Sea Scout Zero, Coastal, Coastal Star and North Sea types.

The NS7 airship illustrated in the painting was a non-rigid of the North Sea type. Twelve of these airships were constructed for the RNAS. With an envelope capacity of 360,000 cubic feet and powered by two 250hp Rolls-Royce engines, the North Sea airships had an endurance of 24 hours and a cruising speed of 58mph.

TRUFLO LIMITED   ERNST & WHINNEY   T.N.T. ROADFREIGHT (UK) LTD

Pears, I.W.M.

**HMS _DUNRAVEN_, VC IN ACTION AGAINST THE
SUBMARINE THAT SANK HER**

This dramatic painting by Charles Pears illustrates the action in which two VCs were awarded, hence the title. HMS _Dunraven_ was a Q-ship disguised as an ordinary merchant vessel. In addition to a 2½lb gun, the normal defensive armament of merchantmen during the First World War, the _Dunraven_ was armed with a 4 inch gun, depth charges and torpedo tubes, all of which were kept concealed.

On 8th August 1917, HMS _Dunraven_ was in the Bay of Biscay steering a zigzag course at eight knots when she was attacked by a German U-boat on

the surface, which opened fire at a range of 5,000 yards. The _Dunraven_ replied ineffectively with her 2½-pounder, until a shell from the U-boat's gun set the stern of the Q-ship on fire. This fire ignited a depth charge which blew up the concealed 4 inch gun. Two 'panic parties' then abandoned ship, leaving the rest of the crew to fight the submarine. With her main armament destroyed, the _Dunraven_ attempted without success to torpedo the U-boat. When a British destroyer came into sight, the U-boat submerged and made good her escape. HMS _Dunraven_ was taken in tow,

but sank before she could be beached.

The commanding officer of HMS _Dunraven,_ Captain Gordon Campbell VC, DSO and bar, was awarded a second bar to his DSO for his part in the action. The first VC was awarded to Lieutenant Charles Bonner RNR for his coolness and skill when under fire from the U-boat, while Petty Officer Ernest Pitcher was selected for his VC. This was unusual in being a Rule 13 award, where an individual is picked from a number of other persons all equally worthy of the award.

Fleming-Williams, I.W.M.

'THE RETURN OF THE RAIDERS, FELIXSTOWE'

In the dramatic painting by C. R. Fleming-Williams, Felixstowe F2A flying-boats are seen returning to the RNAS coastal air station at Felixstowe, Suffolk in 1918 after a patrol over the North Sea.

The F2A was the first of the Felixstowe flying-boats to be extensively used by the Royal Naval Air Service. Among its many roles was that of operating the extremely effective 'Spider's Web' patrol system over the North Sea in the offensive against the U-boat and the Zeppelin. Despite weighing over five tons, F2As took part in many dog-fights with German seaplanes while on patrol. One of the greatest air battles of the war involved the F2A and took place over the North Sea when six enemy seaplanes were shot down.

Although the standard endurance of the F2A was six hours, some flying-boats could stay airborne for over nine hours by carrying extra petrol in cans. Felixstowe F2A flying-boats had a length of 46 feet 3 inches and a wingspan of 95 feet 7 inches. They were powered by two Rolls-Royce Eagle VIII engines, which gave the aircraft a maximum speed of 95 mph.

Among the numerous manufacturers of the Felixstowe F-Type flying-boats was Short Brothers, then a company based at Rochester in Kent.

HMS VINDICTIVE LANDS ROYAL MARINES AT ZEEBRUGGE — 23rd APRIL 1918

During World War I, the Belgian ports of Ostend and Zeebrugge were extensively used by the Germans as submarine bases for their 'U-Boats'. Located on the North European coast, where the English Channel opens out into the North Sea, they afforded easy access to the vital British sea lanes.

Wing Commander F. A. Brock OBE *(left)*

Writing in his memoirs after the war Admiral of the Fleet, Lord Keyes reported that "The value of Brock's contribution to the undertaking was simply incalculable, in addition to fitting out the vessels with smoke-making apparatus, he designed special smoke floats to be anchored in special positions; he also designed immense flame throwers for the Vindictive; parachute flares for aircraft to drop; flare rockets for surface vessels to fire and special light buoys to mark the route. Brock's one plea, which I would have preferred to refuse — as his genius for inventions was so invaluable — was that he should be allowed to take part in the attack". A marine later reported that he had seen Brock, cutlass in hand, searching for what he thought was a new type of German artillery range finder, stationed on the Mole. He was never seen again.

A daring raid, planned by Admiral Sir Roger Keyes with the intention of blocking them, was launched on the 23rd April 1918. It differed from all previous blocking operations carried out by the Navy because it depended for its success upon a smoke screen enabling the slow block ships to reach their correct positions in the heavily defended harbour.

Enough flame to give away the position of a smoke laying vessel had been the achilles heel of all smoke screens up to that time. Wing Commander Brock, of the famous firework company was deeply involved in the planning of the raid and invented a smoke screen so effective that the entire force was able to get within yards of the Zeebrugge harbour guns before it was spotted.

The attack on Zeebrugge led by Captain Alfred F. B. Carpenter, VC RN in HMS *Vindictive* was carried out with enormous heroism, against fierce opposition and heavy enemy fire. Three old minelaying vessels, HMS *Intrepid*, HMS *Thetis* and HMS *Iphignia* were filled with concrete and sunk successfully in the canal as blockships. HMS *Vindictive*, an old cruiser, landed an assault party of seamen and Officers and men of the 4th Battalion Royal Marines on the long Mole. For this operation, *Vindictive*

was held in position by two Mersey ferries, the *Royal Iris* and the *Royal Daffodil,* which had been especially renamed for the action at the express command of HM King George V. This scene, lit overhead by Commander Brock's illuminating rockets, is vividly depicted in the painting by Charles J. de Lacey, which is on display at the Imperial War Museum. An obsolete submarine was used to ram the shoreward end of the Mole and blow it up, so as to cut off the Mole's defenders from any reinforcements.

The battle on the Mole was particularly fierce and crews of the *Vindictive* and the *Royal Iris,* together with the Royal Marines assault parties, carried out the attack with tremendous fortitude. The casualty toll was terrible and there were tales of exceptional heroism. In all, no less than eight Victoria Crosses were awarded, some by ballot, since it proved impossible to choose between the deserved recipients. More than half the Royal Marines embarked and landed became casualties and as a special honour, no other Royal Marine Battalion has ever again been numbered the '4th'.

The Ostend raid failed, since the blockships were all sunk prematurely before reaching their objectives. HMS *Vindictive* set sail again as a blockship for Ostend and her bows may be seen today, as a War memorial in that port.

Frank Mason, I.W.M.

HMS *SUPERB* — BATTLESHIPS INTO CONSTANTINOPLE

The strength of the Royal Navy is well-illustrated in this painting by Frank Mason, as HMS *Superb,* the Flagship of the Commander-in-Chief, Mediterranean leads the British Fleet to Constantinople (Istanbul) in November 1918. When the ships passed the rusting remains of the *River Clyde,* laying where she was beached during the Gallipoli landings in 1915, ensigns were dipped in salute — the ex-collier was sacrificed to provide the

only cover from withering Turkish on-shore fire.

The passage of the British Fleet through the Dardanelles must have been a poignant reminder of the carnage which occurred hereabouts during the early part of the war. Failing to force the narrows of the Dardanelles with warships at the beginning of 1915, it became necessary for the Allies to launch an amphibious landing on the strategically important Gallipoli

peninsula in April 1915. Despite much valiant fighting, the British expeditionary force later had to be evacuated without securing their objective and the sea route through to Constantinople and the Black Sea remained closed until the surrender of the Central Powers in 1918.

BIRDS EYE WALL'S LIMITED

THE END — SIGNING GERMAN SURRENDER

On the afternoon of 15th November 1918, a force of Royal Navy light cruisers and torpedo boats met the German cruiser *Königsberg* near the Inchcape Rock and escorted her through the mists of the North Sea to the RN Naval Base at Rosyth. Aboard the *Königsberg* was a German delegation led by Rear-Admiral Hugo von Meurer. On reaching Rosyth late that evening, the delegation left the cruiser and went aboard the destroyer HMS *Oak,* which conveyed them to the battleship HMS *Queen Elizabeth,* the flagship of Admiral Sir David Beatty, the Commander-in-Chief of the Royal Navy's Grand Fleet. Piped aboard the *Queen Elizabeth,* Rear-Admiral Meurer and his delegation were received on the quarter-deck by Commodore Hubert G. Brand, Captain of the Fleet and escorted below to Admiral Beatty's fore-cabin for initial discussions on the handing over of the German Navy. Three further meetings took place the following day to arrange the final details of the surrender.

In this historic painting by Sir John Lavery, Admiral Beatty is shown reading the surrender terms of the German High Seas Fleet to Rear-Admiral Meurer and four officers of his staff on 16th November.

Frank Mason, I.W.M.

HM SUBMARINE M1 OFF SEDD-EL-BAHR

As HM Submarine M1 passes off Sedd-el-Bahr on the Gallipoli peninsula, she witnesses salvage operations in progress on the rusting hulk of the *River Clyde,* run ashore during the Gallipoli landings in 1915.

When information was received during the First World War that the Germans were building U-boat cruisers fitted with two 5.9 inch guns, the Admiralty decided to order four submarines, each with a 12 inch gun. In the event only three of these large submarines were constructed and were known as the M Class or Monitor submarines. M1 was completed at Vickers in April 1918, nicknamed 'mutton boat', because of her shape, but was never used in action for fear the Germans might copy the idea! The other two submarines were completed in 1920. Five years later both these submarines had their guns removed. M2 was refitted to carry and operate a specially built small reconnaisance seaplane, the Parnall Peto. It was housed in a hangar built forward of the conning tower and was launched by catapult. M3 was converted to a minelaying role; and M4 not completed. The mines were stowed inside a large free-flooding casing on top of the hull, which enabled standard mines to be laid over her stern by chain-conveyor gear. One hundred mines could be carried. M3 was the prototype of the large Seal Class submarine minelayers used by the Royal Navy during the Second World War. Both M1 and M2 were lost in accidents at sea; M1 being rammed in an accident involving the Swedish SS *Vidar* off Start Point on 12 November 1925: there were no survivors, but M3 survived until she was scrapped in 1933. The M Class had a length of 296 feet and displaced almost 2,000 tons when submerged. They had a maximum speed of 14 knots when surfaced.

J.S. CHINN HOLDINGS LIMITED

HM YACHT VICTORIA & ALBERT WITH THE 1st BATTLE SQUADRON, MEDITERRANEAN FLEET AT SPITHEAD DURING THE JUBILEE REVIEW OF 1935

One of the many ships dressed overall.

by kind permission, R. F. Grant.

"At the end of the Review, HM King George V witnessed from HMY Victoria & Albert a concentration shoot by the 15 inch guns of the 1st Battle Squadron against a towed battle-practice target. This painting shows the Royal Yacht leading the Squadron to sea for this demonstration.

The battleships are HM Ships *Queen Elizabeth, Royal Sovereign, Ramillies, Revenge* and *Resolution.*

HMS *Queen Elizabeth* is flying the flag of the Commander-in-Chief, Mediterranean, Admiral Sir William Fisher KCB CVO, and is commanded by Captain S. St. Leger Moore.

HMS *Royal Sovereign* is commanded by Captain B. H. Ramsay, later Allied Naval C-in-C for the invasion of Europe.

HMS *Revenge* is flying the flag of the Admiral Commanding the 1st Battle Squadron, Vice-Admiral C. M. Forbes CB DSO, who was C-in-C Home Fleet at the outbreak of war. The ship is commanded by Captain L. E. Holland who, as a Rear Admiral, was killed in HMS *Hood* when she was sunk by *Bismark.* Midshipman W. D. O'Brien was also on board this ship (*Revenge* — not *Hood!*).

HMS *Resolution* is commanded by Captain J. H. D. Cunningham MVO who became C-in-C Med. in the latter part of the war and then 1st Sea Lord.

The Flag Officer Royal Yachts was Rear Admiral D. B. N. North, CSI CMG CVO. Admiral North became Flag Officer Gibraltar, being relieved of this post in 1940, when soon after the French surrender some units of the French Navy passed through the Straits. Churchill maintained that they should have been intercepted."

Bill O'Brien

Admiral Sir William O'Brien KCB, DSC, who was for many years the guiding light and Chairman of the General Council for King George's Fund for Sailors.

THAMES TELEVISION

John Hamilton, I.W.M.

THE BATTLE OF THE RIVER PLATE

The German pocket battleship, *Admiral Graf Spee,* which had been attacking Allied shipping shortly after the outbreak of World War II, sank two British merchant ships on the 2nd and 3rd December 1939, near the Cape route in the South Atlantic and then proceeded west to the busy shipping route off South America. Before the two ships sank, however, they were able to report the attacks and give their positions.

Commodore H. H. Harwood, flying his pennant in HMS *Ajax,* received news of the sinkings as he sailed north from the Falkland Islands, with HMS *Exeter* and HMNZS *Achilles* and decided to concentrate his force in an area off the River Plate estuary. The force was divided into two divisions, the *Ajax* and *Achilles* in one and HMS *Exeter* in the other. The plan was that, on meeting the enemy, they would attack from different directions.

At about 0600 on 13th December 1939, the *Graf Spee* sighted the three British cruisers and went to action stations; shortly afterwards, HMS *Exeter* reported her to be in sight. A few minutes later, the *Graf Spee* opened fire with her main armament on to the *Exeter* and with her

secondary armament on to the *Ajax* and *Achilles.* HMS *Exeter* immediately altered course to the westward and opened fire, whilst *Ajax* and *Achilles* made for the other side of the *Graf Spee,* opening fire soon after. Within an hour, HMS *Exeter* had been hit several times, her forward turrets and bridge were out of action and very serious fires had started on board. However, *Exeter* had managed to hit the *Graf Spee* a number of times, before being forced to break off the action at about 0730 and had also made a determined but unsuccessful torpedo attack on the enemy. Meanwhile, the *Ajax* and *Achilles* had closed with the *Graf Spee* and scored a considerable number of hits. *Ajax* fired her torpedoes, but they were avoided by the enemy. Both *Ajax* and *Achilles* were damaged and when *Ajax's* after turrets were put out of action at 0740, Commodore Harwood decided to break off the action and shadow the German ship. HMS *Exeter* with a list to starboard and down by the bows, was ordered to return to the Falklands for repairs.

The Captain of the *Graf Spee,* Captain Langsdorff, decided that, in view of the severe damage to his ship and the great distance from his home bases,

he would make for Montevideo and get permission from the Uraguayan Government to stay there long enough to make the necessary repairs to his ship. Early in the morning of 14th December, the *Graf Spee* anchored off Montevideo and *Ajax* and *Achilles* patrolled outside the harbour, in international waters. Additional support was on the way; HMS *Cumberland* from the Falklands and HMS *Ark Royal,* HMS *Revenge* and three cruisers were steaming down from the north. Captain Langsdorff had hoped that the Uraguayan Government would allow him to stay in harbour longer than the 72 hours laid down by international law. In spite of strong pressure from the German Ambassador, this the Uraguayan Government refused to allow. The necessary repairs could not be carried out within the stipulated time limit and on Sunday evening the 17th December 1939, the *Graf Spee* put to sea. Shortly after 2000, two explosions shook the ship and a flash of flame leapt skywards as she blew herself up. The *Graf Spee* had been scuttled by her Commander on the express orders of Hitler; Captain Langsdorff committing suicide ashore in his ship's battle ensign.

HMS *ROYAL OAK* IS SUNK AT SCAPA FLOW

Shortly after the outbreak of World War II, at 1.30 am, during the silent hours of 14th October 1939, the British battleship HMS *Royal Oak* was sunk by the German submarine U 47 (Lieutenant Priem), as she lay at anchor in Scapa Flow. So sudden was the attack that it resulted in the loss of 833 officers and men.

The U 47 braved the tides and currents during that night as she entered through the Holm Sound, the eastern entrance to the anchorage, and the narrow passage between the two block ships in the Kirk Sound to sight her prize, the *Royal Oak*. Soon after, a salvo of torpedoes was fired at the battleship; only one, however, hit her in the bow, causing a muffled explosion.

So incredible was it to the Admiral and Captain on board that a torpedo could have struck them in the safety of Scapa Flow, the explosion was at first attributed to some internal cause. Several minutes later, the U 47 fired another salvo and three of the four torpedoes struck the ship and ripped her bottom out. In ten minutes, she capsized and sank. Most of the crew were at action stations, but the rate at which the ship turned over made it almost impossible for anyone below to escape. Shortly after, the U 47 crept quietly away, through the eastern entrance, to the North Sea.

The attack at Scapa Flow and the loss of HMS *Royal Oak* caused instant reactions in the Admiralty and the scale of the defences for Scapa Flow were greatly increased. A plaque in memory of those who lost their lives in the ship was placed by the Admiralty in the ancient Cathedral of St. Magnus in Kirkwall.

The *Royal Oak* was built in the Naval Dockyard at Devonport and first commissioned in May 1916. As one of the five Royal Sovereign Class battleships she took part in the Battle of Jutland, 1916. To many who served in her she was known as the "Mighty Oak". She was the eleventh ship to bear the name. The first was built in 1663, to commemorate the tree in Shropshire in which King Charles II hid after the Battle of Worcester in 1651.

Michael Turner.

Wilkinson I.W.M.

THE LITTLE SHIPS OF DUNKIRK

From 26 May, until 4 June 1940, there took place what was described in an Admiralty communique as "The most extensive and difficult combined operation in British naval history" — the evacuation of the British Expeditionary Force from Dunkirk, codenamed "Operation Dynamo".

A fleet of no less than 222 British naval vessels and 665 other craft took part in this maritime drama. The latter were manned largely by crews comprised of fishermen, yachtsmen and members of the Royal Naval Volunteer Reserve. Many, undismayed by enemy fire as their boats were sunk or abandoned, transferred to other vessels to continue the work of rescue. The incredible armada of small craft included pleasure yachts and tiny rowing boats, Thames tugs and paddle steamers, Dutch motor vessels left in British ports after the German invasion of Holland and even the

London Fire Brigade river float *Massey Shaw,* which besides ferrying over 500 men from shore to the waiting transports, herself made the double cross-Channel journey twice, each time with sixty men aboard. Royal Navy vessels deployed included the Cruiser *Calcutta,* with destroyers, a sloop, corvettes, minesweepers and gunboats. French, Dutch and Polish ships also took part. Of the naval vessels engaged, only six destroyers and twenty-four minor craft were lost, though throughout every moment, the operation was hampered by incessant bombing attacks from the air and heavy bombardment from the German land batteries on shore.

The troops waded out to meet the small boats, which then carried them to the larger craft used as transports, which had to lie outside the shallows some half-mile from the shore, where they were easy targets for submarine

and torpedo boat attacks. Meanwhile, British naval forces shelled enemy shore batteries to protect the flanks of the withdrawing troops and Hurricanes and Spitfires of the RAF battled with aircraft of the Luftwaffe above the turmoil of the crowded beaches.

This marvellous feat of skill and bravery by Servicemen and civilians alike, crowned, in the words of King George VI "by a success greater than we had dared to hope", will live forever in the annals of British history. In a matter of seven days, a total of 224,585 British, together with 112,546 French and Belgian troops were evacuated. The men of Britain's army were saved as though by a miracle, but not so their equipment, arms or stores.

Dorothy Wilding

King George VI, president 1917-1936, KGFS.

CROUZET LIMITED   TRAGO MILLS GROUP   YEWLANDS ENGINEERING CO. LTD.

C. Cundall: I.W.M.

THE DUNKIRK WITHDRAWAL FROM THE BEACHES

On 30th May 1940, news of one of the most amazing military operations of all time was made known to the world. Many British, French and Belgian troops had reached the tiny French Channel port of Dunkirk and were already being evacuated from the beaches by a flotilla of 887 craft, both naval and civilian of every size and shape. From 30th May until 3rd June, over 336,000 men in all reached safety. In the painting, troops can be seen on the sands, wading out waist-deep to meet the little boats, that will convey them to the rescuing ships, and drawn up on the beach awaiting the strange navy, gathering to take them to safety. The fires of furiously burning petrol tanks in the town are creating a huge pall of smoke

in the background and during the entire time of their long wait to be rescued the men on the beaches were subjected to almost continuous bombing and machine attacks from German planes. Casualties might have been considerably more serious were it not for the British fighters and anti-aircraft batteries which engaged the raiders on the outskirts of Dunkirk.

Waiting their turn to find places in the rescue vessels, the troops at Dunkirk scattered over the neighbouring sand dunes, taking such rough cover as they could find and went down to the beach in batteries as boats became available. Chains of men, neck-deep in water and many still with their rifles and equipment, waded out from the shore to scramble up the

sides of the rescue ships to be hailed by such ironic cries from those already aboard as "Keep your socks dry!".

Many of the little boats used in the Dunkirk operation were manned by amateur crews and came from the Thames and the coast towns of Southern and South East England. A Thames boat firm acted as a clearing house, collecting small craft of all kinds, especially motor boats and their crews from London's River. The RNVR played an important role in these vital operations. Many of the small craft were damaged or sunk, but most returned to await the resumption of their calmer life as pleasure boats.

Robert Taylor. In the collection of the Military Gallery, Bath.

HMS GLORIOUS WITH SWORDFISH AIRCRAFT AND DESTROYER ESCORT

HMS *Glorious,* one of the early class of aircraft carriers in the Royal Navy, was originally built as a light battle cruiser by Harland and Wolff, Belfast and entered service in 1917. She was fitted with three twin 15 inch guns and carried aircraft for flying off the gun turrets. At the end of World War I, she was placed in the Reserve Fleet in 1919. In 1924, the Admiralty decided that *Glorious* and her sister ship HMS *Courageous* should be converted into aircraft carriers. *Glorious* was taken out of the Reserve Fleet and moved to the Naval Dockyard at Devonport for her conversion; she was completed and re-commissioned in early 1930.

At the outbreak of World War II, *Glorious* was attached to the Mediterranean Fleet and in 1940 returned to the Home Fleet where she was based at Scapa Flow. In May of that year, the evacuation of the Allied Forces from Narvick in Norway was underway and on 31st May, *Glorious* sailed from Scapa Flow to Narvick to pick up RAF Gladiator and Hurricane aircraft, which had been operating there. The destroyers HMS *Acasta* and HMS *Ardent* accompanied her as an anti-submarine escort. For some time, British ships had been operating in the area, independently,

in the absence of any direct threat from the German Navy.

Early on the 8th June, the RAF aircraft had been flown aboard the *Glorious* and she set course for Scapa Flow at 17 knots. Unknown to the British Forces, Flag-Officer Narvik, the Commander-in-Chief Home Fleet, the German battle-cruisers *Scharnhorst* and *Gneisau* were operating in northern waters. At 1600, they were sighted by *Glorious* and she went to action stations. *Acasta* and *Ardent* made for the enemy and laid down a smoke screen, which delayed their gunfire for a short while, but *Glorious* was completely outranged. After sustaining very serious damage and with heavy fires burning in several places, *Glorious* sank at about 1740. *Acasta* was sunk shortly before *Glorious,* but *Ardent* was still capable of action and was close enough for her to fire her torpedoes, one of which hit the *Scharnhorst* before *Ardent* too was sunk.

The torpedo hit severely damaged the *Scharnhorst* and reduced her speed, so the German battle-cruisers abandoned their operations and returned to Trondheim.

THE SWORDFISH   RICHARD WILSON.

This Fairey Swordfish Mk.2 LS326; known affectionately as stringbags, belongs to the Royal Navy's Historic Flight, based at Yeovilton. It was built by the Blackburn Aircraft Company in 1943 and was presented to the Royal Navy in 1960 by the Fairey Aviation Company.

Robert Taylor. In the collection of Mr. and Mrs. Robert James.

The destroyer HMS Kelly steaming into action during World War II.

HMS KELLY — CONTACT BEARING 190

HMS *Kelly* was named after Admiral Sir John Kelly and was launched by his daughter. On 23rd August 1939, ten days before the outbreak of World War II, she was handed over by her builders, Hawthorne Leslie, to her Commanding Officer, Lord Mountbatten, who had been appointed Captain (D) commanding the 5th Destroyer Flotilla. All of the ships of the Flotilla were brand new vessels of the 'J' and 'K' Class and HMS *Kelly* was the Flotilla Leader. The *Kelly* was, from the first, a happy and efficient ship and the teamwork, engendered by Mountbatten, enabled the commissioning time to be cut from the usual three weeks down to three days.

One of HMS *Kelly's* first missions was to sail to Cherbourg and return to Portsmouth, carrying the Duke and Duchess of Windsor back from France

to the safety of the United Kingdom. In December 1939, Mountbatten was ordered to collect every available destroyer in the Tyne and search for a German U-Boat, which was believed to have torpedoed four ships in the River estuary. During this operation, HMS *Kelly* struck a mine, which fortunately did not explode until hit by her propellors, but she had to be towed back and repaired.

The next time that the *Kelly* was in trouble was during the Norwegian campaign, when she was ordered to intercept and sink some German minelayers. Whilst heading at full speed for her target, *Kelly* was hit by a torpedo and had to be taken in tow by HMS *Bulldog,* a destroyer from another flotilla. In spite of further attacks by both German E-Boats and the Luftwaffe, *Kelly* arrived home to Hawthorne Leslie's Yard at Hebburn on the Tyne after ninety-two hours in tow. HMS *Kelly* was again repaired and recommissioned in November 1940 and many of her old ship's company rejoined her.

In 1941, HMS *Kelly* was despatched to the Mediterranean and in the May of that year, she sank the last of the 'caique' invasion fleet and successfully

bombarded Maleme airfield in Crete. Following this action, HMS *Kelly* was herself attacked, during the Battle of Crete, by twenty-four Junkers 87 Stuka dive-bombers and turned over whilst steaming at 34 knots. More than half of the *Kelly's* officers and men were lost and the survivors, oil-smeared and burnt, were machine gunned in the water whilst clinging to the only raft to remain afloat. Nevertheless, they still found enough voice to cheer the *Kelly* as she finally went down and Lord Mountbatten is reputed to have said: "We didn't leave the *Kelly,* the *Kelly* left us!".

The story of the *Kelly* during the first twenty-one months of the War was told by Noël Coward, a great friend of Lord Mountbatten, in his classic film "In Which We Serve". Names, places and situations were changed at Mountbatten's request, but the *Kelly's* exploits were the inspiration for the film.

The story of HMS *Kelly* is not particularly remarkable, when set against the background of other heroic events of World War II. What singled her out was the exceptionally high morale of her ship's company under the leadership of her distinguished and respected Captain.

BELFAST CAR FERRIES LIMITED   MMM CONSULTANCY GROUP LTD   THE TAUNTON CIDER COMPANY

SUBMARINES IN THE SECOND WORLD WAR

During the Second World War, HM Submarines operated in every area of Naval operations throughout the world and played a notable role in bringing victory. In the conflict at sea, British submarines sank almost two million tons of Axis shipping and although no capital ships were sent to the bottom, many smaller warships including 35 submarines were destroyed. In addition to their normal role, the Silent Service took part in many special operations of a cloak and dagger nature. Submarines were also responsible for towing X-Craft (midget submarines) and carrying human torpedo chariots to within striking distance of their targets.

In this photograph taken in 1942, submarine *Seadog* (P216), a Sealion Class built under the Emergency War Programme, is seen in company with *Thunderbolt* (N25) in the Holy Loch, Scotland. On the after casing of *Thunderbolt* can be seen two containers used for transporting human torpedo chariots. This submarine was originally the *Thetis,* which sank with heavy loss of life before the war and was subsequently salvaged and recommissioned. In 1943, *Thunderbolt* was lost while on patrol in the Mediterranean, an area in which she operated human torpedo chariots with some success.

CLYDE PORT AUTHORITY   HARRISON (CLYDE) LTD   JAMES BUCHANAN & CO LTD

HMS *FORTH* — AND WINSTON CHURCHILL VISITS HOME FLEET

.Taken during the middle of the war, in this photograph three of HM Submarines are seen alongside the submarine depot ship HMS *Forth*. Completed in 1939 just before the outbreak of war, the 9,000 ton *Forth* was over 500 feet in length and was capable of carrying out most large repairs on submarines. She was equipped with heavy and light machine work-shops, a foundry and specialised trades workshops. The depot ship would have supplied the submarines with their munitions (including torpedoes), fuel, food and mail. Also shown in the photograph is an Officer of the Sealion Class HM S/M *Sibyl,* as he steps aboard HMS *Forth*.

The Prime Minister, the Rt. Hon. Winston Churchill MP with the Lord Privy Seal, Sir Stafford Cripps, and the Commander-in-Chief Home Fleet, Admiral Sir John Tovey, 11th October, 1942.

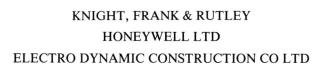

KNIGHT, FRANK & RUTLEY

HONEYWELL LTD

ELECTRO DYNAMIC CONSTRUCTION CO LTD

W. Wilkinson, I.W.M.

RE-BOARDING THE TANKER 'SAN DEMETRIO'

On 5th November 1940, a thirty-eight ship convoy, under the protection of the armed merchant cruiser *'Jervis Bay'*, was attacked in the North Atlantic by the German battle-cruiser, *'Admiral Scheer'*.

Amongst the ships making up the convoy was the motor ship *'San Demetrio'*, a tanker owned by the Eagle Oil & Shipping Company (which merged with Shell Tankers in 1960). The ill fated *San Demetrio* left Aruba in September 1940, carrying some 11,200 tons of vitally needed petroleum and joined the convoy at Halifax, Nova Scotia, before it set sail on 28th October.

When the convoy came under attack, *Jervis Bay* gallantly turned to engage the more powerful enemy vessel and ordered the convoy to scatter. In spite of the attacker's far heavier armament, *Jervis Bay's* Commander, Captain Fogarty Fegen RN, gave battle. Though she was heavily hit and set on fire early in the action, the *Jervis Bay* closed with the *Admiral Scheer* and managed to hold the German fire long enough to enable most of the convoy to escape. After about three hours, *Jervis Bay* sank, but, because of her action, 32 ships of the convoy managed to reach port safely. Her Captain was posthumously awarded the Victoria Cross for his splendid action.

Unfortunately, the *'San Demetrio'*, having set course for home, was again intercepted by the *Admiral Scheer* and set on fire. Her Master, Captain G. Waite OBE, ordered her crew to abandon ship and they took to the boats.

Two days later, No.1 boat, with Second Officer A. H. G. Hawkins in charge, sighted the still burning *San Demetrio* and despite the imminent danger of an explosion, managed to re-board her. The dramatic painting by W. Wilkinson vividly depicts this brave event. The sixteen men, including only two engineers, were able to put out the fires and restart the ship's engines, after an heroic struggle.

The *San Demetrio's* bridge had been destroyed. There were no charts, radio or navigating equipment but by the most skilful seamanship, Second Officer Hawkins brought the vessel home to the Clyde where she was able to deliver 11,000 tons of the original 11,200 tons of her vital cargo. In recognition of his gallantry, Second Officer Hawkins was deservedly awarded the OBE. The *San Demetrio's* Master and the remainder of the crew were safely rescued and taken to St. John's, Newfoundland.

Later in World War II, on 17th March, 1942, while under command of Captain C. Vidot OBE, the *San Demetrio* was torpedoed by the German submarine U404 and sank 80 miles east of Chesapeake Bay.

SHELL TANKERS (UK) LIMITED

Robert Taylor, The Military Gallery.

HMS ILLUSTRIOUS — MALTA 1940

HMS Illustrious — Portsmouth 1986
Built 1982

Battle honours: Genoa 1795;
Basque Roads 1809; Java 1811;
Taranto 1940;
Mediterranean Convoys 1940-41;
Malta Convoys 1941; Salerno 1943;
Sabang 1944; Palembang 1945;
Okinawa 1945.

HMS *Illustrious*, the aircraft carrier of World War II fame, was accepted into service in May 1940 and shortly afterwards she joined the Naval Fleet operating in the Mediterranean.

In November 1940, Fleet Air Arm aircraft operating from HMS *Illustrious* and HMS *Eagle* took part in the Battle of Taranto and carried out a sensational torpedo attack on the Italian Battlefleet, which was anchored, behind powerful defences, in the harbour. The attack was carried out at night and three enemy battleships and two cruisers were badly damaged and put out of action for some time.

Early in 1941, *Illustrious* was hit by German Stuka dive-bomber aircraft, while operating west of Malta, but managed to get into Grand Harbour, Malta, for repairs. She was again heavily attacked, whilst under repair, but after several days, was able to slip away to Alexandria and then on to the USA for a major refit.

In the Spring of 1942, the *Illustrious* sailed to the Indian Ocean and

joined the Far Eastern Fleet. In the May of that year, together with HMS *Indomitable*, she provided air-cover for the landing of Allied forces in Madagascar. Early in 1943, after a brief period in the UK, she rejoined the Fleet in the Mediterranean where she took part in the naval operations covering the landings in Sicily and on the Italian mainland.

She rejoined the Far Eastern Fleet for a period in 1944, before joining the British Pacific Fleet to take part in operations with the US Navy. In April 1945, she returned home for a major refit and in 1946 took on the duties of a trials carrier.

HMS *Illustrious* was built by Vickers-Armstrong at Barrow and had a standard displacement of 23,000 tons, a length of 745 feet and a beam of 95 feet. Sixteen 4.5 inch anti-aircraft guns in twin turrets were fitted on either side of the flight deck and a number of smaller guns were also carried. Thirty-six aircraft could be stowed in the heavily armoured hangar.

FLEET AIR ARM ATTACK ON TARANTO

On the night of 11/12 November 1940, a brilliantly planned and executed attack was made by 21 Swordfish aircraft, from the aircraft carriers HMS *Eagle* and HMS *Illustrious,* on capital ships of the Italian fleet, at anchor in Taranto harbour.

Originally, that attack was planned for Trafalgar Day — 21 October — but had to be postponed due to an accidental hangar fire on board *Illustrious.* Then the *Eagle* was found to have her aircraft fuel supply contaminated by seawater and was withdrawn at the last minute. Five of her aircraft from 813 and 824 Squadrons transferred to *Illustrious* to join the attack with the aircraft of 815 and 819 Squadrons already embarked on *Illustrious.* Eventually, HMS *Illustrious,* commanded by her Captain Dennis Boyd RN and with Rear Admiral Lyster, the originator of the plan, embarked set sail with the Mediterranean Fleet from Alexandria.

Last minute reconnaisance photographs showed not only the disposition of the Italian Fleet, but also the formidable enemy defences, including a balloon barrage and anti-torpedo nets around the larger ships.

At 1800, when the Mediterranean Fleet was to the west of the Island of Zante, HMS *Illustrious* was detached with an escort of cruisers and destroyers to the flying-off point. The 21 Swordfish aircraft took off in two waves, an hour apart. The first wave was airborne at 2057 at a position some 170 miles distance from Taranto. The attack was pressed home with bombs and torpedoes against fierce defensive anti-aircraft fire from the Italian ships and shore batteries. From beginning to end, the first torpedo strike lasted only five minutes. After it, the 35,000 ton battleship *Littorio* was baldy damaged and the 23,000 ton *Cavour* was sinking. The bombing attack took longer and after the final wave of aircraft completed their assault, they left two battleships *(Littorio* and *Cavour)* partly under water, another battleship *(Caio Duilo)* severely damaged, two cruisers badly listing

to starboard and two fleet auxiliaries with their sterns under water. Subsidiary attacks also succeeded in setting fire to oil storage tanks and wrecking the sea-plane base. Only two British aircraft were lost in the entire action.

Admiral Cunningham, Commander in Chief Mediterranean Fleet, wrote of the attack — "Taranto and the night of 11/12 November 1940, should be remembered forever as having shown, once and for all, that in the Fleet Air Arm, the Navy has its most devastating weapon. In a total flying time of about six and a half hours — carrier to carrier — twenty aircraft had inflicted more damage upon the Italian Fleet that was inflicted upon the German High Seas Fleet in daylight action at the Battle of Jutland".

The benefits of Taranto were seen quite quickly and its result decisively altered the balance of naval power in the Mediterranean.

John Hamilton, I.W.M.

MINESWEEPERS UNDER ATTACK

Vividly illustrated in the painting by John Hamilton are Junkers 87 dive bombers which can be seen attacking minesweeping trawlers in the Thames estuary during October 1940. Minesweepers were frequently subjected to air attacks, especially in the waters off south east England, and along the east coast, as air cover could not always be provided.

At the beginning of the Second World War, both Britain and Germany laid prodigious quantities of mines and during the first four months of hostilities, 79 Allied merchant ships were sunk by hitting enemy mines in home waters. To increase the Royal Navy's minesweeping capability, fishing trawlers were requisitioned and converted to the minesweeping role. Despite the extra flotillas so provided and the frequency of the minesweeping operations conducted in home waters, the thousands of mines laid by German aircraft, submarines and coastal forces took their toll of Naval and merchant shipping. But our ports and coastal shipping lanes remained open throughout the period of hostilities.

(Right): A mine-laying trawler in action, HMT *Sapphire.* By Robert Taylor.

ASSOCIATED FISHERIES plc

THE BATTLE OF MATAPAN

On March 27th 1941, a Royal Air Force Sunderland flying boat, on a reconnaisance patrol, reported that it had sighted a large Italian naval force south of Sicily, heading east towards Crete and the area crossed by British convoys taking supplies to Greece. The force was comprised of the battleship *Vittorio Vineto*, several cruisers and a number of destroyers, formed up into two groups.

On receiving this information, the Commander-in-Chief, Mediterranean Fleet, Admiral Sir Andrew Cunningham, in his flagship HMS *Warspite*, with HMS *Barham* and HMS *Valiant*, the aircraft carrier HMS *Formidable* and a number of destroyers, left Alexandria that evening and sailed north west to engage the enemy. South of Crete, a light cruiser force, consisting of HMS *Orion* (Vice-Admiral H.D. Pridham-Wippell), HMS *Ajax*, HMS *Gloucester* and HMAS *Perth* and four destroyers was on patrol to prevent any attacks on allied shipping going to Greece.

Early in the morning of the 28th March, the Italian force was reported to be south of Crete, steering south-east. Shortly afterwards, the *Orion* Squadron made contact with the enemy force and turned to the east to lure them towards the main Fleet, coming from Alexandria and about 90 miles away. They managed to keep the range open, but were subjected to some very heavy gunfire from the *Vittorio Vineto*.

About noon, the first torpedo attack by Fleet Air Arm aircraft from HMS *Formidable* was lauched and the Italian force, which put up a very heavy anti-aircraft barrage, altered course and retired to the north-west. Further attacks by *Formidable's* aircraft were made in the afternoon and at least one direct hit was scored on the *Vittorio Vineto* and she was seen to be stopped for a time, before getting underway again and heading towards Italy at reduced speed. One more attack was made from HMS *Formidable* before the night set in and the cruiser *Pola* was hit and stopped, badly damaged and out of action.

As the British ships pursued the enemy to the west, the night engagement developed, south of Cape Matapan. HMS *Orion*, ahead of the main fleet, reported ships to port and at about 2230 HMS *Warspite*, HMS *Valiant* and HMS *Barham* sighted the Italian cruisers *Fiume* and *Zara* heading east to the assistance of the disabled *Pola*. Both of the Italian cruisers were overwhelmed by the heavy close-range gunfire from the British battleships and the *Fiume* sank shortly afterwards. The *Zara* was later sent to the bottom by torpedoes from HMS *Jervis*. The accompanying Italian destroyers carried out a torpedo attack against the British battleships, but it was avoided and three destroyers were sunk. Greek destroyers helped in the action and tried to cut off the Italian retreat.

The disabled Italian cruiser *Pola* was still laying helpless and stopped and HMS *Havock* went alongside and took off some 260 members of her crew. Early in the morning of the 29th March, *Pola* was sunk by torpedoes from the British destroyers. A large number of Italian survivors from the other cruisers which had been sunk were picked up at dawn by other destroyers, but these were withdrawn when German dive-bombers arrived on the scene. Admiral Cunningham then decided to withdraw his ships and return to Alexandria; though attacked by German aircraft on the way back, no British ships were lost during the operations. Before leaving the battle area, Admiral Cunningham sent a signal to the Italian Naval HQ, suggesting that a hospital ship be sent to pick up the remaining Italian survivors, still in the water, and for this he was thanked by their Commander-in-Chief.

John Hamilton, I.W.M.

Battle of Matapan — Warspite and Valiant surprise the enemy.

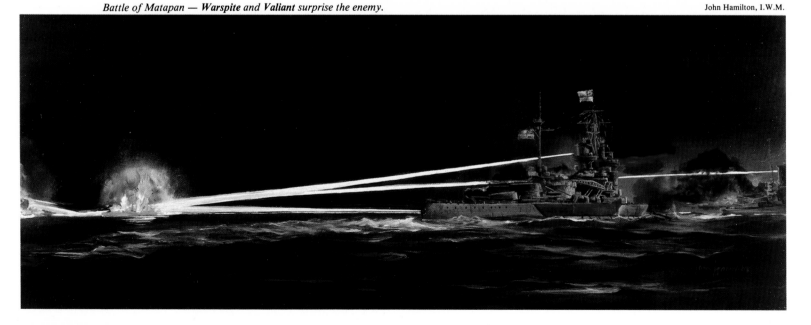

John Hamilton, I.W.M.

THE EVACUATION OF CRETE — 1941

At the end of April 1941, the German armed forces were in control of the mainland of Greece and many of the islands in the Aegean Sea. The island of Crete was, however, still being defended by British, New Zealand and Greek forces and the Cretan Islanders themselves. The ships of the Mediterranean Fleet, operating in the area in support of our forces, also used the anchorage in Suda Bay.

It was clear that the Germans would soon attack the island to gain a very strategic position in the eastern Mediterranean. After heavy bombing attacks on the British bases at the western end of the island, the expected assault was launched with an air-borne attack, in great strength, supported by troop landings on the coast on 20th May 1941, in the Carnia and Suda Bay area. Despite determined resistance by the Allied forces and aircraft, the powerful enemy units advanced steadily eastwards across the island, under cover of almost complete air superiority. By 27th May, it was decided that the immediate withdrawal of our forces from Crete was imperative, in order to avoid further losses, and the orders for the evacuation were issued.

The evacuation took place during the next few days and at first, the Allied naval forces were able to take off many troops who were in the Candia and Retino areas, despite being heavily attacked by the Germans. As the German force moved along the northern part of the island, the Allied troops were forced to retreat, over the mountains, to the south coast. The evacuation continued from the beaches on the south coast of the island under continuous and heavy attack by the Germans, who had a vast superiority in the air. The intensity and drama of these attacks is well captured in the vivid painting by John Hamilton. Despite these attacks, however, about 18,000 Allied troops were got safely away to Egypt, but unfortunately many had to be left behind.

During this operation, the cruisers HMS *York*, *Gloucester* and *Fiji* and the destroyers HMS *Kelly*, *Juno*, *Greyhound*, *Kashmir*, *Imperial* and *Hereward* and a number of merchant ships were lost. Several others were badly damaged, including the aircraft carrier HMS *Formidable*. *Formidable* had carried out a bombing raid on a Luftwaffe airfield near Crete and on her return to Alexandria was heavily bombed by German aircraft from North Africa. The Greek Navy and Merchant Service also suffered heavily during the evacuation.

NIARCHOS (LONDON) LIMITED

Alan Fearnley, P.G.Av.A.

SUNDERLAND AT SCAPA

The original of this painting, which was painted by Alan Fearnley for the Guild of Aviation Artists, is on display at the Fleet Air Arm Museum at Yeovilton in Somerset. It depicts a Short Sunderland flying boat of RAF Coastal Command overflying Royal Navy battleships, anchored at Scapa Flow during World War II.

Throughout the war years, a close bond developed between the men of the Royal Navy and those of RAF Coastal Command. The sight of a friendly Sunderland flying overhead was always a most welcome one to those on board the ships in the North Atlantic convoys.

The Short Sunderland was developed just before the war from the Short "Empire" class passenger flying boat and first entered service with the RAF in 1938. The Sunderland was well equipped with a heavy defensive armament and carried depth charges for use against enemy submarines. Sunderlands flew on anti-submarine patrols over the North Atlantic, often in terrible weather and without sighting a German U-Boat. However, when an enemy submarine was sighted, the action was often brief, as the submarine hurriedly crash-dived.

In 1943, the German submarines started mounting multiple 20mm and 37mm cannons in their conning towers and the U-Boat Commanders would then often opt to remain surfaced and fight it out with the flying boats. The Sunderlands were very vulnerable to attack from below and several were lost in these anti-submarine actions, whilst trying to protect the convoys.

Reproduced by kind permission of Vickers plc.

HMS *KING GEORGE V*

The battleship HMS *King George V* (known affectionately as *KGV),* was built by Vickers Armstrong on the Tyne. She was commissioned in December 1940 and joined the Home Fleet at Scapa Flow.

Early in 1941, she took the new British Ambassador, Lord Halifax, to the United States of America and on the return voyage, escorted a convoy to the United Kingdom. Shortly afterwards, the *King George V* was part of the naval force covering the Commando landings in the Lofóten Islands and was also involved in the search for the German battleship *Scharnhorst,* which had been attacking allied shipping in the Atlantic before eventually being forced to retreat to Brest.

In April 1941, the *King George V* became the Flag Ship of the Commander-in-Chief Home Fleet, Admiral Sir John Tovey, and in May of that year, she took part in the search for and the eventual sinking of the German battleship *Bismark*. During 1942 and early 1943, she was involved

in the search for the German pocket battleship *Admiral Scheer* in the North Atlantic and protecting Allied shipping to and from the northern ports of Russia.

In 1943, *King George V* left the Home Fleet and went to the Mediterranean to join 'Force H' in covering the landings on Sicily and on the mainland of Italy, taking part in the occupation of the Italian naval base at Taranto in September. She then returned to the UK, was refitted for service in the Far East, and joined the British Pacific Fleet, Force 57, in December 1944. During 1945, wearing the flag of Vice-Admiral Sir Bernard Rawlings, commanding the British Force 57, she took part, together with the United States naval forces, in covering the air strikes on the Japanese islands of Ryukus in March and the Sakishima group in May. She was also involved in the bombardment of Hitachi and areas of Honshu and Hamamatso on the mainland of Japan in July.

HMS *King George V* was present in Tokyo Bay, when Japan formally signed the instrument of total surrender aboard the American battleship USS *Missouri.* Admiral Sir Bruce Frazer, the Commander-in-Chief British Pacific Fleet, signed for Great Britain.

On her return to the United Kingdom, HMS *King George V* became the Flagship of the Home Fleet, until she was later placed in Reserve and eventually disposed of in 1957.

The *King George V* Class of battleships included HMS *Duke of York,* HMS *Anson* and HMS *Howe.* These had a displacement of 35,000 tons and were 740 feet in length and 103 feet beam; they carried a total complement of 1,900 officers and men. Their armament comprised ten 14 inch guns in three main turrets of which two had quadruple mountings; sixteen 5.25 inch guns; 60-90mm pom-poms; 8-40mm and 28-20mm cannons.

VICKERS plc

**SWORDFISH TORPEDO BOMBERS TAKE OFF FROM
HMS ARK ROYAL — 1941**

Robert Taylor. In the collection of The Fleet Arm Museum.

Swordfish torpedo bombers of the Fleet Air Arm flew on many historic naval actions during World War II. Among these were the virtual destruction of the Italian Fleet at Taranto in 1940, the glorious and gallant attack on the German battle cruisers *Scharnhorst* and *Gneisnau* during their famous Channel dash in 1942 and the sinking of the elusive German battleship *Bismarck* in 1941.

The Swordfish, built by Fairey Aviation had a wing span of 45' 6" and a length of 36' 1". She was powered by a Bristol Pegasus 30 engine of 750hp and was capable of a maximum speed of 138mph and a range of 750 miles. Her stalling speed was 59mph. The Swordfish's armament consisted of a .303 Vickers machine gun, an 18" torpedo, or mines or rockets or depth charges. She carried a crew of three.

After the sinking of HMS *Hood* by the *Bismarck* on 24th May 1941, the British Home Fleet, now bent on revenge, continued to chase the German battleship. Force H, comprising the battleship HMS *Renown,* the aircraft carrier HMS *Ark Royal* and the cruiser HMS *Sheffield* was despatched from Gibraltar to reinforce the Home Fleet. On the night of 24th May, the *Bismarck* was hit by a torpedo from a Swordfish aircraft from HMS *Victorious* and then early next morning, contact was lost. On 26th May, *Bismarck* was again located, 550 miles west of Lands End, by a Catalina flying boat of RAF Coastal Command. *Bismarck* drove the Catalina off with her anti-aircraft guns, but a Swordfish aircraft from HMS *Ark Royal,* which was now within flying distance, continued to shadow her. Meanwhile, Force H continued to steam from the south-east into a furious easterly gale, which had prevailed for several days. Not only was *Bismarck* running low on fuel, so also was the Home Fleet. Personal orders from Winston Churchill to "sink the *Bismarck*" had to be obeyed; an attack by the Fleet Air Arm was the only hope.

That evening, in the most appalling weather conditions, a strike of fifteen Swordfish aircraft of 810, 818 and 820 Squadrons, Fleet Air Arm, took off from *Ark Royal.* In conditions of mountainous seas, with the flight deck heaving and falling, they flew off to rendezvous with the cruiser HMS *Sheffield,* which had earlier been attacked herself, in error, by the same aircraft, due to the atrocious weather conditions, fortunately with no ill effect.

This second strike was successful, and *Bismarck* was severely damaged by torpedoes aft, reducing her speed and crippling her steering. This air attack enabled the battleships HMS *King George V* and HMS *Rodney* to establish contact on the morning of 27th May. The gunfire of these two British capital ships silenced the *Bismarck* and the Commander-in-Chief Home Fleet ordered HMS *Dorchester* to send her to the bottom with torpedoes. *Bismarck,* ablaze from bow to stern, went down with her colours flying, having withstood a battering unprecedented in the annals of naval warfare.

The Chase of Bismarck

GREENLAND

Bismarck first sighted 2032 23 May

Norfolk and Suffolk

ICELAND

Hood sinks 0630 24 May

Hood and Prince of Wales

Aircraft from Victorious attack 0200 25 May

Action with Prince of Wales 1840 24 May

King George V

Contact lost 0300 25 May

Rodney

Noon 25 May

0900 25 May

1100 26 May

Sighted by RAF 1030 26 May

Aircraft torpedo attack from Ark Royal 1930 26 May

Destroyer attack 0130 27 May

Sinks 1100 27 May

0   500
miles

Robert Taylor. Mr. Alan Bryce.

THE GERMAN BATTLESHIP 'BISMARCK'

Pride of the German navy at the start of World War II, the *Bismarck* was a mighty battleship. She had a displacement of 41,700 tons and her main armament comprised eight 15-inch guns, in four twin turrets, two fore and two aft; her secondary armament consisted of twelve 5.9-inch guns and sixteen 4.1-inch anti-aircraft guns. Although she was a floating fortress of armour plate and massive fire power, her deck armour was badly placed to deal with either bomb damage or plunging shellfire and in her last action, she very quickly succumbed to British shells.

On 21st May 1941, her Captain, Admiral Lütjens took her out of the safety of the Norwegian fjords at Bergen, into the open North Sea. Three days later, on 24th May, she was intercepted by the British Navy and during the ensuing battle, the *Bismarck* landed a direct hit on the British battleship HMS *Hood,* sinking her in one mighty explosion. Damaged herself, *Bismarck* made for St. Nazaire for repairs, but was spotted by a Catalina

flying-boat of the RAF, some 700 miles west of Brest. Shortly afterwards, Swordfish aircraft, flying from HMS *Ark Royal,* severely damaged *Bismarck's* rudder and propellors with torpedoes, but she managed to survive the day.

The next morning, 27th May 1941, *Bismarck* was confronted by units of the Home Fleet, including the battleships HMS *Rodney* and HMS *King George V.* Unable to steer properly, the *Bismarck* fought a gallant rear guard action, but the odds against her were too great and after two hours of furious battle she was sunk by a torpedo fired from the cruiser HMS *Dorsetshire,* and went down burning from end to end. Thus ended an epic piece of Naval history. In Robert Taylor's painting, he depicts the *Bismarck* firing a broadside from her forward guns, during the course of her final combat.

John Hamilton.

THE 'SCHARNHORST' AND 'GNEISNAU' IN CHANNEL DASH

Lt.-Cdr. Eugene Esmonde VC.

Since mid 1941, the German battlecruisers *Scharnhorst* and *Gneisnau,* both of a standard displacement of 26,000 tons and with a primary armament of nine 11 inch guns, together with the cruiser *Prinz Eugen* had been sheltering in the French port of Brest. They had been constantly under attack by the RAF, who had dropped more than 4,000 tons of bombs on them, but had nevertheless remained afloat. Since the Germans had evidently been able to make good any damage, it was decided to try and get these important ships back to their bases.

After dark, on the night of 11th February 1942, the *Scharnhorst, Gneisnau* and *Prinz Eugen* slipped out of Brest and made a spectacular escape up the English Channel to German ports. Helped by bad weather, they had a strong escort and were protected by a huge air umbrella mounted

by the Luftwaffe from shore bases, as they steamed up the Channel at a speed about 30 knots, close to the French coast.

They were first sighted at 1100 by patrolling RAF fighters as they were approaching the narrows of the Straits of Dover. An attack was immediately launched and six Fleet Air Arm Swordfish torpedo-reconnaisance bombers of 825 Squadron, under Lieutenant Commander A. Eugene Esmonde DSO RN, flew out from the RAF Station at Manston, escorted by a large number of fighters. They attacked the enemy at mast height in the face of a furious anti-aircraft barrage and not one of the Swordfish aircraft returned. Lieutenant Commander Esmonde was posthumously awarded the Victoria Cross, the first to be won by the Fleet Air Arm in World War II. The other four Officer survivors were each awarded the DSO and Leading Airman

Bunce the Conspicuous Gallantry Medal. The eleven members of 825 Squadron who did not return were mentioned in Despatches. Vice-Admiral B. H. Ramsey, the Flag Officer Commanding Dover, commenting on this tragic piece of human endeavour wrote: "In my opinion, the gallant sortie of these six Swordfish constitutes one of the finest exhibitions of self-sacrifice and devotion to duty that the war has yet witnessed".

As the German ships got clear of the Dover Straits and headed for their ports, Royal Navy destroyers and motor-torpedo boats carried out several attacks, but to no avail, since the enemy E-boats had laid a heavy smoke-screen. Air attacks were also kept up in great strength. However, the *Scharnhorst* and *Gneisnau* both struck mines, which had been laid ahead of them, before they finally reached their German bases.

TRUSTHOUSE FORTE plc   H.P. BULMER HOLDINGS plc   MOTOROLA MILITARY AND AEROSPACE

John Hamilton.

SS OHIO REACHES MALTA — THE PEDESTAL CONVOY

In the middle of 1942, the Island of Malta was facing a desperate situation due to the tremendous pressure being put on it by the German and Italian air forces. In August of that year, "Operation Pedestal" was mounted to get a convoy of fourteen large, fast, merchant ships, carrying vital supplies, through to the Island from the west. The escorting forces included battleships, cruisers, destroyers and an aircraft carrier.

The convoy included the SS *Ohio,* a large, 14,000 ton tanker, belonging to the Texaco Oil Company of America, which had been chartered by the British Ministry of War Transport, especially for this convoy, to carry an exceptionally vital cargo of aviation spirit to the beleagured Island. She was placed under the management of the Eagle Oil and Shipping Company and was manned by Captain D. W. Mason as Master and a specially selected British crew. A team of naval ratings and soldiers was also carried to man the anti-aircraft guns.

On Saturday night, 8th August, the convoy and its escort forces slipped through the Straits of Gibraltar, under the cover of darkness, and proceeded towards its destination at a speed of fifteen knots. The forenoon of the 11th August saw the first action, when the aircraft carrier HMS *Eagle* was

tragically sunk by a U-boat. From then on, the expected air attacks began and the convoy was under almost continuous attack by aircraft, U-boats and E-boats until it reached Malta. The *Ohio* was singled out for heavy attacks, and one night was hit by a torpedo and forced to stop. Steering by hand from aft, she somehow caught up with the convoy the next day. During the continuous air attacks concentrated against the *Ohio,* the ship was straddled by a stick of bombs, which almost lifted her out of the water. Eventually, a bomb exploded in her boiler room and she was again brought to a stop. Temporary repairs were achieved and the *Ohio* struggled on. A Stuka dive-bomber aircraft shot out of control and crashed on her deck. She was once more hit by a bomb, which put the engines out of action and she was then taken in tow. Twice she was abandoned and twice re-boarded. However, the end of this long drawn-out ordeal was approaching and British aircraft from Malta were beginning to provide air cover, but she was not home yet!

At dawn on 14th August, a near miss carried away the SS *Ohio's* rudder and holed her aft, but with two destroyers either side and one ahead she was got underway again. While the AA gunners aboard the tanker and the

destroyers fought off the divebombers, the crew worked desperately to keep the ship afloat. As Malta came in sight, naval tugs came out to give assistance to the gradually sinking ship. As day dawned on 15th August, the SS *Ohio* was literally carried into Valetta harbour between two destroyers, where she received a tremendous welcome. When the last of her precious cargo was pumped out, she settled down on the bottom of the harbour.

Operation Pedestal enabled Malta to survive and regain her critically important position in the Mediterranean. Five of the fourteen merchant ships in the convoy reached Malta, but in spite of the loss of HMS *Eagle* the cruisers HMS *Manchester* and HMS *Cairo* and a destroyer, a heavy toll was taken of the enemy submarines and E-boats.

Captain D. W. Mason, Master of the *Ohio,* was awarded the George Cross, in recognition of his personal courage and determination and that of every member of his crew. In 1946, the hulk of the *Ohio* was towed out of Valetta harbour and sunk in deep water off Malta — a fitting burial ground for such a great ship.

THE GALLANT *TEKOA*

When Convoy HX229 sailed from Canada bound for the United Kingdom in March 1943, no fewer than 40 German U-boats were waiting to intercept it in the Atlantic. At the same time a westward-bound convoy left Britain and as the two convoys converged, they offered the U-boat packs many easy targets. During the ensuing engagement, one of the largest of the war, 21 Allied ships totalling 141,000 tons were sunk, for the loss of just one U-boat.

In this dramatic painting by John Hamilton, the SS *Tekoa* owned by the New Zealand Shipping Company lies stopped at the height of the action in order to rescue survivors from the sinking merchantmen SS *Nariva,* the American freighter *Irene du Pont* and the blazing oil tanker *Southern Princess.* With ships being torpedoed all around her, the *Tekoa* managed to rescue 145 survivors from the three ships in the most hazardous circumstances. The lack of rescue ships in the convoy caused agonising decisions to be made by the Naval escorts as to whether to stop and pick up survivors or to attack the U-boat contacts. It was almost suicidal for a merchant ship to stop and be left behind on her own.

March 1943 proved a disastrous month for the Allies, with 77 ships being sunk by U-boats in the Atlantic. But by the summer of 1943, the turning point in the Battle of the Atlantic had been reached and slowly shipping losses decreased, while the number of U-boats destroyed jumped dramatically. During 1943, some 237 U-boats were sunk, the majority by shore-based aircraft.

John Hamilton, I.W.M.

John Hamilton, I.W.M.

SNOWBERRY — DOMINION LINK IN
THE BATTLE OF THE ATLANTIC

His Majesty's Canadian Ship *'Snowberry'* was one of the scores of Royal Canadian vessels which made their contribution, in the face of the enemy and the elements, to keeping Britain's lifeline to the North American Allies open during the darkest days of the War. In fact, hardly a convoy sailed without a Canadian corvette's protection to shepherd its merchant flock's progress through the wolfpacks lying in wait off the North American coast, including the Newfoundland ports. This was often an arduous and undramatic task involving long hours at sea in all weathers, but cramped the U-Boats' style and at the limit of their seagoing endurance, made life more difficult for them. And sometimes it brought more obvious and real victory as when *'Snowberry'* sank U-536 in November 1943.

BAIN & COMPANY (SECURITIES) LTD

BANK OF NEW ZEALAND

PEAT MARWICK, MITCHELL & CO

John Hamilton IWM.

THE S.S. *REGENT LION*

The Battle of the Atlantic was at its height in the Spring of 1941. The war against Britain's merchant convoys in the Atlantic was much intensified in the March and April of that year and in those months, British and Allied shipping losses rose to 489,299 tons and 488,124 tons respectively, representing a total of no fewer than 255 vessels lost. Though they were protected by the Allied Navies and the Royal Air Force, to the best of their ability, the men of the Merchant Navy had no alternative but to sail in all weathers, keep strictly to their convoy positions and formations and avoid unnecessarily manoeuvring their ships in order to evade the enemy.

During the early years of the Battle of the Atlantic, the centre of that unfriendly ocean was completely out of range of Allied air cover. This fact made it impossible to effectively control the attacks of the German U-Boats, especially with the acute shortage of suitable naval escorts for the merchant convoys.

Until 1943, the losses of merchant ships, especially tankers, was far in excess of the rate of replacement. The balance was not redressed until the Liberty Ships and other prefabricated vessels, hurriedly produced in large numbers by the tremendous efforts of American and Canadian shipyards, became available. Because of this, the salvage of damaged merchantmen was attempted wherever possible. This was the case with the SS *Regent Lion,* owned by The Bowring Steamship Company Ltd. *Regent Lion* was torpedoed in the South Western Approaches in 1942 and was towed into Falmouth and repaired. She was torpedoed again at the entrance to the Strait of Gibraltar and once more a fight began to save her, as shown in John Hamilton's dramatic painting. Ignoring danger from the tanker's cargo of petrol, the coal-burning anti-submarine trawler *Arctic Ranger* came alongside to assist with the tow. However, despite great courage and effort, SS *Regent Lion* was blown ashore near Europa Point at Gibraltar.

The bravery of the merchant seamen, who served in the tankers knowing that one U-Boat torpedo could turn them into a sudden mass of flame, should never be forgotten.

C.T. BOWRING & CO. LTD

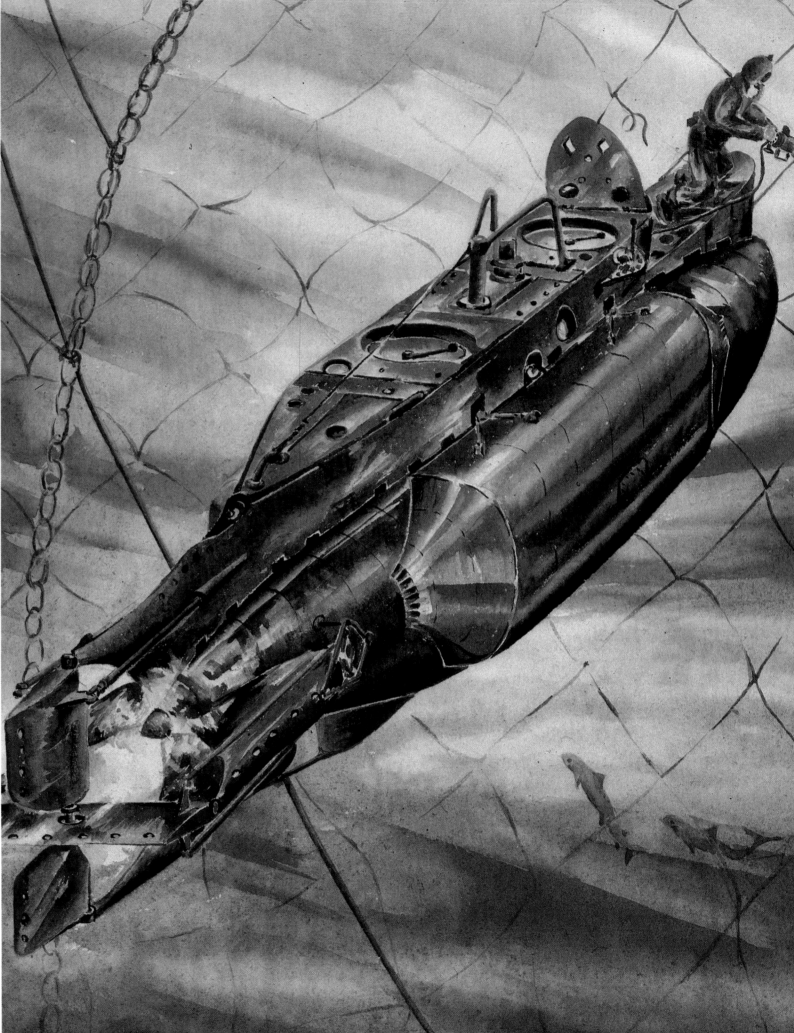

MIDGET SUBMARINE ATTACK ON 'TIRPITZ'

During 1943, the German battleship *Tirpitz,* based in the Alten Fjord in northern Norway, was a constant threat to Allied shipping, on its way to the Russian ports. She was attacked on several occasions by aircraft of the Royal Air Force, Fleet Air Arm and the Russian Air Force and was finally sunk in an attack by the RAF in November 1944.

One of the well remembered and most daring operations, which put the *Tirpitz* out of action was carried out by *X-craft,* midget submarines of the Royal Navy, in September 1943. These little *X-craft,* each with a crew of three, were fitted to carry a two-ton charge of high explosive on either side. Six were detailed for the operation and on 22nd September 1943 were towed from their base in Scotland, across the North Sea, to the entrance to Alten Fjord. Only four arrived, one being lost when her tow parted and one having to be scuttled when she had to jettison her charges due to air leaks.

The *Tirpitz* was moored behind strong net defences around 50 miles up a heavily guarded channel at Kaafjord, at the inshore end of the Alten Fjord. Nevertheless, of the four *X-craft* which managed to get up the channel, *X-6* and *X-7* laid their charges under the *Tirpitz. X-5* was probably sunk by gunfire, before she could make her attack, and the other craft, *X-10,* developed serious defects which could not be rectified in sufficient time for her to make the attack; she was the only one to return to her base.

The *Tirpitz* was seriously damaged by this attack, but managed to escape more serious damage by moving her bows away from the charges, having sighted one of the *X-craft* and recognised the danger, before the charges were due to explode. The captains of *X-6* and *X-7,* Lieutenant D. Cameron RNR and Lieutenant B. C. G. Place were each awarded the Victoria Cross for their gallantry in the attack and for the measures they took for the safety of their crews, when they scuttled the *X-craft* to prevent them falling into enemy hands, before they were taken prisoners.

The *X-craft* midget submarine was 40 feet in length and of 35 tons, with a crew of three. They carried two large detachable side charges, each containing two tons of explosive, fired by a time fuse. The method of attack was to proceed submerged into the enemy harbour and dive beneath the selected target, releasing the charges directly under the hull. They would then withdraw and after a predetermined time, the charges would explode, blowing a large hole in the bottom of the enemy ship. The *Tirpitz* was, in fact, rendered unfit for sea until April 1944.

J. Brooks, I.W.M.

JANE HODGE FOUNDATION

John Hamilton, I.W.M.

NIGHT BATTLE — MTB'S IN ACTION

In the dramatic night-time painting by John Hamilton, Royal Naval light coastal forces are intercepting a German inshore convoy off the French coast in 1944. This fierce action would have lasted no more than a very few minutes.

The German convoys were moved along the Channel and North Sea coasts almost entirely by night and usually in short stages from one port to the next. They were protected by trawlers and larger vessels heavily armed as flak ships and despite these screening escorts, our light coastal forces would make repeated forays against the enemy convoys. Our motor

torpedo boats and motor gun boats relied on their speed and surprise of attack to avoid serious damage. MTBs were fitted with a torpedo tube mounted on each side of the deck amidships, firing forwards and had a maximum speed of nearly 50 knots. During the latter part of the war, many were adapted as motor gun boats in order to deal with the threat posed by German E-boats. MGBs were used to protect our own coastal convoys and were also employed in the offensive role.

Our coastal forces were mostly manned by the Royal Naval Volunteer Reserve and many MTBs and MGBs were commanded by RNVR officers.

ALLIED-LYONS plc

A Royal Marine Flotilla of Landing Craft Assault (LCA's) forming up in the Channel on the night of 5th June, 1944.

for the Fleet. This made a total of one hundred and sixty-eight Fleet Air Arm aircraft involved in the operation.

The dive bomber crews had been practising on a dummy range in Scotland, which bore a resemblance to *Tirpitz's* mooring in Kaa Fjord and had reached a high degree of efficiency. On 30th March 1944, the carriers sailed with the Home Fleet from Scapa Flow and for once the Arctic weather was bright and clear. The flying off position, 120 miles north-west of Kaa Fjord, was reached in the early hours of 3rd April, by which time the final briefings were taking place and the aircraft had been bombed up. This part of the operation is shown in the photograph and was no small problem, given the 1600lb armour-piercing bombs, two varieties of 500 pounders and the then new 600lb A/S bombs.

Shortly after 0400, in ideal flying conditions, the aircraft were airborne. A little after 0500, about 25 miles off the Norwegian coast, they climbed to 10,000 feet; they passed Alta and Läng Fjords, where the fighters jettisoned their long-range fuel tanks and then turned eastwards to Kaa Fjord, with its steep sides protecting *Tirpitz's* narrow anchorage.

The enemy were taken completely by surprise and no hostile fighters appeared. German sailors were seen still running to action stations when the first bombs from the Barracudas hit the *Tirpitz*. Within minutes, by 0530, the attack was over. Out of twenty-one Barracudas attacking, nine scored direct hits and five achieved near misses. Back on the carriers, the second strike wave was flying off. They too were successful, in spite of the

I.W.M.

FLEET AIR ARM PERSONNEL PREPARE FOR A RAID ON THE 'TIRPITZ'

The German battleship *Tirpitz,* sister ship to the *Bismark,* posed a significant threat to the convoys that started to sail to Russia, following her invasion by Germany in 1941. As a result of the gallant attack by midget submarines in September 1943, *Tirpitz* had been out of action for six months, in Kaa Fjord, Norway.

A strike by the Fleet Air Arm was subsequently mounted, when it was known that the *Tirpitz* was ready for sea again. Planned long before, this strike was known as 'Operation Tungsten'. Armed with a variety of

FAA Museum.

bombs, of up to 1600lbs, were forty-two Barracuda aircraft of 827, 829, 830 and 831 Squadrons, Fleet Air Arm. These aircraft were accompanied by twenty-eight Corsairs of 1834 and 1836 Squadrons, twenty Hellcats of 800 and 804 Squadrons and forty Wildcats of 881, 896, 882 and 898 Squadrons. They were flown off the Fleet Carriers HMS *Victorious,* and HMS *Furious* and the Escort Carriers *Emperor, Pursuer* and *Searcher.* Twelve Swordfish aircraft, eight Wildcats from HMS *Fencer* and eighteen Seafurys from HMS *Furious,* provided air and anti-submarine protection

element of surprise now being lost. By 0800, all aircraft were on board and 'Operation Tungsten' was over. Fourteen direct hits had been scored on *Tirpitz* for the loss of three Barracudas and their crews and a Hellcat. As a result of this well planned and successfully executed attack, *Tirpitz* was out of action for a further three months, bringing precious time for the Arctic convoys.

It is worthy to note, that of the 163 aircrew involved, no fewer than 138 were Reserve personnel, most seeing action for the first time.

I.W.M.

HMS *HOWE* PASSES THROUGH THE SUEZ CANAL

The picture shows HMS *Howe,* the flagship of the Commander-in-Chief of the Pacific Fleet, Admiral Sir Bruce Fraser, passing through the Suez Canal on her way to join the Pacific Fleet in June 1944. She is painted in the Admiralty Disruptive camouflage scheme in use at that time. In the foreground can be seen an Egyptian Felucca.

HMS *Howe* was one of the King George V Class of battleships. She was built at the Fairfield Yard on the Clyde and commissioned in August 1942 when she joined the Home Fleet at Scapa Flow.

Her early operations with the Home Fleet involved the escorting of Allied convoys to and from the northern ports of Russia. In March 1943, the *Howe* sailed to the Mediterranean to join 'Force H' and she played an important part in covering the Allied landings on Sicily and on to the mainland of Italy.

In June 1944, HMS *Howe* joined the East Indies Fleet, based at Trincomalee in Ceylon (known today as Sri Lanka). She remained there for a short period before proceeding to join the newly formed British Pacific Fleet, known as 'Task Force 57' in December, as the flagship of the Commander-in-Chief. During 1945, she took part in a number of operations, together with the United States Navy, against the Japanese in the Formosa and Okinawa campaigns. HMS *Howe* returned to the United Kingdom in January 1946, after a refit in South Africa, and became a training ship, before being placed in Reserve. HMS *Howe* had a displacement of 35,000 tons and was 740 feet in length and 103 feet in the beam; she carried a complement of 1,900 Officers and men. Her armament comprised ten 14 inch guns in three turrets (two of which were a quadruple mounting), sixteen 5.25 inch guns, 60-90mm pom-poms, 8-40mm guns and 28 20mm guns. HMS *Howe* was sent for disposal in 1958.

ROYAL NAVY DIVERS CLEAR SUEZ MINES

In the late summer of 1984, a series of underwater explosions damaged more than twenty merchant ships along the Suez Canal and the Red Sea. These were believed to have been caused by the unlawful laying of terrorist mines along the shipping lanes of this politically unstable area and an international force was mustered to clear them.

Royal Navy minehunters had been exercising in the Mediterranean since April and a task group comprising the four Royal Navy minehunters HMS *Kirkliston* commanded by Lt. D. R. Long RN, HMS *Gavinton* (Lt. N. A. Bruen RN), HMS *Bosington* (Lt. G. P. Johnson RN), HMS *Brinton* (Lt. N. J. Ford RN) sailed from Taranto on 9 August 1984. They were accompanied by the support ship *Oil Endurance* and the whole group was under the command of Commander John Porter RN. After stopping off at Akrotiri in Cyprus to pick up stores and fuel, they passed through the Suez Canal on the night of 14 August, just ahead of a squadron of French MCMVs.

On arrival at Adabiya Naval Base in Suez Bay, degaussing and acoustic ranges were set up and Trisponder precise navigation stations were set up along the coast, to enable the minehunters to exactly fix their positions during the operations.

By 17 August, the first ships, now under overall command of Commander Tony Chilton RN, were on task and on 29 August they were joined by HMS *Wilton* (Lt. S. D. McAlear RN). The ships were supported by the Fleet Clearance Diving Team, equipped with remote control submersibles fitted with underwater searchlights and low-light TV cameras capable of taking underwater video film. They operated at the top of the Gulf of Suez in an area covering some 150 square miles of international shipping routes, and further support was provided by the staff of the British Embassy naval attache in Cairo.

A World War II 500lb bomb and a German GC ground mine were located and destroyed, also an 18 inch practice torpedo.

Other unusual objects located included oil drums, a kitchen sink, metal pipes and boxes, aircraft wings, a pair of train wheels, two engine turbines and a ship's anchor and a toilet.

On completion of the operation, the area covered was truly clear of underwater hazards and free to navigation of those busy international shipping lanes.

DPR (N) M.o.D.

Michael Turner.

Burma 1945. Battle of Kangaw — Royal Marine Commandos take cover as a Japanese machine gun opens up from the bushes above their heads during the attack on hill 170.

JAPANESE 'KAMIKAZE' ATTACK ON A BRITISH AIRCRAFT CARRIER

It was early in 1945, just before the close of hostilities in Europe, that the British Pacific Fleet, chiefly comprising heavy aircraft carriers, joined up with the United States Pacific Fleet at Okinawa. The British Fleet was commanded by Admiral Sir Bruce Fraser, operating mainly from Sidney, Australia and from Guam. Commanding at sea was Vice-Admiral Sir Bernard Rawlings, in HMS *King George V,* and commanding the aircraft carrier squadron was Admiral Sir Philip Vian. This squadron comprised the carriers HMS *Indefatigable, Illustrious, Victorious* and *Indomitable,* each with about sixty aircraft on deck. During the Okinawa campaign, the role of this force, known first as Task Force 57 and then Task Force 37, was to keep the Japanese air forces on Formosa from supporting their army in Okinawa.

The Japanese response to the attack on Okinawa was almost entirely a matter of Kamikaze suicide attacks from the air on the US and British Fleets. The Kamikazes made ten main attacks in April, May and June 1945, as well as many minor attacks. Over 1,400 suicide planes took part in the main attacks and they were accompanied by a similar number of bombers. They damaged the American Admiral Spruance's flagship *Indianapolis* so severely that he transferred his flag to the battleship *New Mexico,* which was in turn also hit by a Kamikaze on 12th May. On 6th/7th April 1945, some 355 Kamikazes and 341 other aircraft attacked the combined fleet. They sank three destroyers, an LST and two freighters, laden with ammunition. They also damaged seventeen other ships, some so severely that they were immediately scrapped at the end of the war.

Each of the British aircraft carriers was damaged quite badly by the Kamikazes. After about two weeks, *Illustrious,* still bearing the scars of an earlier campaign, was replaced by HMS *Formidable* and in June 1945, HMS *Implacable* joined the Pacific Fleet. In July and August, these ships joined the attacks on the Japanese mainland.

Royal Marines of the British East Indies Fleet after landing at Port Swettenham, Penang, off the coast of Malaya in 1945. LSI ***Princess Beatrix.***

John Worsley.

BRITISH NAVAL OFFICER PoWs ON A FORCED MARCH FROM BREMEN TO LUBECK IN APRIL 1945

From left to right: Lieut. John Worsley RNVR, Naval War Artist; Lieut. "Butch" Hain RN (Fleet Air Arm); Lieut. Robert Staines RNVR; Lieut. Bill Mewes RNVR; Ober-Lt. Schoof, in charge of march.

The Naval prison camp was Marlag 'O' at Westertimke, thirteen miles S.E. of Bremen and it took some two weeks to make the journey of eighty miles to Lubeck.

During the march the column was attacked by British fighters who could not see the Union Jack displayed over their cart shown on the left of the picture. Six officers were killed.

Along the way German farm hausfraus were glad to swap old prams for Red Cross chocolate and cigarettes and two prams are shown being used to carry belongings.

In the right centre is depicted Lieut. Bill Mewes RNVR who escaped in 1944 through 'Albert', the dummy officer constructed and worked by Lieut. John Worsley RNVR with the assistance of Lieut. Bob Staines RNVR who is depicted in the centre with Mewes.

Mewes was away from Marlag for three weeks before unfortunately being recaptured by the Gestapo after a Swedish Captain at Lubeck refused to take him on board.

Many readers may have seen the film "Albert RN" which gives a very accurate account of the actual escape although the storyline woven around it is fictitious.

On the far left is depicted John Worsley, who was an Official Naval war artist when captured in the Adriatic. He is carrying three metal tubes made from Klim milk tins hammered end to end which came in Canadian Red Cross parcels. In these he carried out all his drawings and paintings done in the camp: he painted this scene and wrote this caption.

RCA SYSTEMS LTD   RCA SERVICES LTD   RCA OPERATIONS LTD

Robert Taylor. In the collection of The Fleet Air Arm Museum.

THE PUTTALAM ELEPHANTS

During the latter part of World War II, the Fleet Air Arm established a number of land-based Air Stations, located in jungle clearings, to support air operations against the Japanese in the Indian Ocean and Pacific theatres of war.

One such air base was HMS *Rigolia,* situated at Puttalam in Ceylon (now Sri Lanka), about 75 miles north of Colombo. The airfield at Puttalam consisted of an open circle, cut out of the jungle, with a single runway made out of "Somerfeld" steel-strip tracking, running down the centre. On the seaward side, the airfield was lined by a row of tall palm trees, which could be a 'dicey' hazard to pilots taking off in no wind conditions. The other three sections of the circle were lined by dense jungle and off the runway

was sand, which very quickly turned into thick mud, after rain.

Following a rain shower, which would be a frequent occurrence, the steel strips of the runway rapidly became very slippery and the whole runway surface turned into an 'ice rink'. No matter how much flying skill was applied, landing conventionally in these conditions was an impossible business. All that a pilot could do was to stamp on the brakes, lock the wheels and allow the Corsair aircraft to slide gracefully into the muddy sand alongside the runway. This having been safely accomplished, the call then went up for the duty elephant! One was named 'Fifi' and had this painted in white letters, amidships, on her side. The elephant duly appeared, guided by her mahout, who sat high up on it's neck, clad only in

his loincloth.

To get the aircraft back on to the runway, ropes were fixed to the elephant's collar and the other ends tied around the under-carriage legs of the Corsair, just above the wheels. With a little encouragement from her mahout and available aircrew, the elephant slowly hauled the aircraft back on to the runway, from the opposite side, since it did not like padding around on the slippery steel tracking. To have carried out this task by any other means would have taken many hours and much effort.

The Puttalam elephants were also employed to tow the petrol bowsers, which were used for refuelling the aircraft.

THE LIFE AND TIMES OF A DESTROYER — IN WAR, INSURRECTION & PEACE

HMS *Cavalier,* a destroyer of the Fleet C's (Caesar) Class, was laid down in February 1943, launched on 7 April 1944 and completed one year and nine months later on 22 November 1944. She was built and engined by J. S. White and Co, Cowes, Isle of Wight; standard displacement 1,710 tons, length 363 feet, breadth 36 feet and with armament of $4 \times 4.5''$ single, 2×40mm Bofors, 4×20mm Oerlikons in twin power mountings and 2×20mm Oerlikons single.

Joining the 6th Destroyer Flotilla, *Cavalier* took part in three operations off Norway: striking at enemy shipping, providing cover for a minesweeping flotilla and joining convoy RA 64 on 23 February 1945 which had been attacked by U-Boats and enemy aircraft and forced to scatter, but only three ships were lost before it reached the Clyde on 1 March. She was then ordered to join the British Pacific Fleet, but by the time she had refitted at Rosyth that conflict too was over. Her Battle Honour 'Arctic 1945'. During the next 28 years of a remarkably long career, Cavalier was to visit virtually every part of the globe. She started

with India in February 1946 as a show of force in the face of unrest in that country's Navy and apart from periods in the Reserve and refits, including a major modernisation at Thorneycrofts in Southampton which brought her up to date with postwar naval developments, she served extensively in the Far East, was often the guard ship at Gibraltar, took part in many of the NATO and SEATO exercises of her day and in December 1962 rushed the Queen's Own Highlanders and their equipment to Brunei where an armed rebellion there and in North Borneo had resulted after the formation of Malaysia. And in 1963 was part of the Royal Tour to Australia. She had earlier been part of the Christmas Island Atomic tests force and thereafter in 1959 was sent to guard RAF installations during unrest on their staging post of Gan Island. She was also engaged in the Bahamas patrol during the Castro take-over in Cuba, and later on the blockade of Beira during that stage of Rhodesian developments. Numerous goodwill visits were made to various countries, including the Scandinavians and those of the Eastern Mediterranean. Amongst other incidents, whilst accompanying *Eagle* she

saved the life of a Greek merchant seaman by rushing him to Gan's Hospital and in September 1970 she took in tow, as salvage, the *Saint Brandan* which was ablaze and drifting abandoned and brought her into Milford Haven. In 1972 she was berthed alongside *Belfast* in the Pool of London on a 'Meet the Navy' visit and on 5 July that year she returned to Chatham for the last time, officially 'approved for disposal'. On 21 October 1977 *Cavalier* was formally handed over to the HMS *Cavalier* Trust, who had bought her to be a floating museum dedicated to the ubiquitous destroyer and her role in the 20th Century Royal Navy, before these charasmatic little ships, even audibly different with their distinctive 'bark', disappeared forever into the anonymity of the multi-purpose 'Type' classes of the seventies and eighties.

Tugs of Alexandra Towing took her first to Southampton and on 22 November 1983 to her present berth in Brighton Marina and honourable but still useful retirement.

BRENT WALKER HOLDINGS plc   **THE BRIGHTON MARINA COMPANY LIMITED**

HMS *BELFAST*

Robert Taylor. In the collection of Mr. G. Bryan.

The Cruiser, HMS *Belfast* was built by Harland & Wolff in the City from which she took her name and was commissioned into service in August 1939. She joined the 18th Cruiser Squadron just before the commencement of World War II. In November 1939 she was transferred to the 2nd Cruiser Squadron, based at Rosyth and on the 21st of that month was extensively damaged by a German magnetic mine in the Firth of Forth. As a result, she had to be almost entirely rebuilt before rejoining the Home Fleet at the end of 1942.

HMS *Belfast* then took part in escorting convoys to Russia and played a key role in the Battle of the North Cape in December 1943, which ended in the sinking of the German Battle Cruiser *Scharnhorst*. In June 1944, *Belfast* led the cruiser bombardment in support of the Allied landings in Normandy on D-Day. Between 1945 and 1947 she was flagship of the 5th Cruiser Squadron based in Hong Kong. She returned to Portsmouth at the end of 1947 for a long refit and was placed in the Reserve Fleet.

In 1949, HMS *Belfast* was again the flagship of the 5th Cruiser Squadron in Hong Kong at the time of the *"Amethyst"* incident. She also provided fire support for the United Nations Forces throughout the Korean War. After an extended refit at Devonport, she returned to the Far East as Flagship of the Station in 1960. Her active career ended in 1963.

The last survivor of the Royal Navy's big ships, who's main armament was guns, HMS *Belfast* is now permanently moored in the River Thames, opposite the Tower of London, as a floating museum. She is the first warship since HMS *Victory* to be preserved for the nation. In 1967, the Imperial War Museum initiated efforts to save the warship from the scrapyard and in 1971 the 'HMS *Belfast* Trust' was formed. It was in the October of that year that she was opened to the public.

When HMS *Belfast* was built she had a standard displacement of 11,500 tons, an overall length of 614 feet and a beam of 66 feet. Her armament comprised twelve 6 inch guns mounted in four triple turrets, twelve 4 inch anti-aircraft guns, a number of smaller close-range guns and two triple torpedo mountings. Two Walrus aircraft were also carried.

HMS Amethyst.

GALLAHER LIMITED

Richard Wilson.

FAIREY FIREFLY AS5 WB271 AND
HAWKER SEA FURY FB11 TF956

Fairey Firefly AS5 WB271 and Hawker Sea Fury FB11 TF956 form part of the Royal Naval Historic Aircraft Flight based at the Royal Naval Air Station at Yeovilton in Somerset. The Flight can frequently be seen giving flying displays at airshows all over the country during the summer months.

The Firefly was used extensively as a carrier-borne fighter/reconnaissance aircraft during the latter half of the Second World War and in the Korean War. Together with the Sea Fury, it had a remarkable record

of reliability. The Sea Fury was the Fleet Air Arm's last piston-engined fighter in front line squadrons, where it served from 1947 until 1954.

Fairey Firefly AS5 WB271 served with the Royal Navy and the Royal Australian Navy before being put up for disposal. She was subsequently purchased by the officers of the aircraft carrier HMS *Victorious*, then on a visit to Sidney and presented to the Fleet Air Arm Museum in 1972 and restored to flying condition in the same year.

Hawker Sea Fury FB11 TF956 was built in 1947. She went to Korea in HMS *Warrior* and joined 807 Squadron aboard HMS *Theseus* late in 1950, flying a total of 213 hours operationally while the carrier was in Korean waters. TF956 was presented to the Fleet Air Arm Museum in 1971 and restored to flying condition in the following year.

THE ASSOCIATED OCTEL CO LTD

HMS *VANGUARD*

HMS *Vanguard,* the last battleship to serve in the Royal Navy, was built by John Brown & Company of Clydebank. She was launched in 1944, but by then, her completion was no longer a wartime priority and she eventually entered service in 1946. She had a displacement of 44,000 tons, with a length of 815 feet and a ship's complement of 1,900 Officers and men. Her armament consisted of eight 15 inch guns in four twin turrets; sixteen 5.25 inch dual-purpose guns and seventy 40mm Bofors Anti-aircraft guns. The 15 inch guns were originally mounted in HMS *Courageous* and HMS *Glorious* and were removed when they were converted into aircraft carriers in 1924-1930. HMS *Vanguard* was finally broken up for scrap at Faslane in 1960.

During her brief career, HMS *Vanguard* had the honour of taking HM King George VI and HM Queen Elizabeth on a Royal Tour to South Africa in 1947. She was the Flagship of the Home Fleet Training Squadron in 1949 and served in the Mediterranean and the Atlantic. In 1953 *Vanguard* was present at the Coronation Review of the Fleet at Spithead, for HM Queen Elizabeth II. Between 1956 and 1960 she was the Flagship of the Flag Officer, Reserve Fleet at Portsmouth.

The name *"Vanguard"* has been used nine times in the Royal Navy and dates back to 1586, when a galleon-type ship of 32 guns bearing the name was launched at Woolwich. She took part in the campaign against the Spanish Armada in 1588 and was present at the sacking of Cadiz in 1596. The third *Vanguard,* launched in 1678, took part in the Battle of Barfleur in 1692. The fifth *Vanguard* was a third-rate, 74 gun ship, built at Deptford in 1787 and was Lord Nelson's Flagship at the Battle of the Nile in 1798. The eighth *Vanguard* was a dreadnaught of 19,250 tons which took part in the Battle of Jutland in 1916 but in 1917 she blew up at Scapa Flow due to overheated magazines.

VANGUARD UNIT TRUST MANAGERS LIMITED

Richard Wilson.

SEA VIXEN REFUELLING

Two Hawker Siddeley Sea Vixen FAW1 aircraft carry out a flight refuelling exercise accompanied by a Sea Vixen FAW2.

Developed from the de Havilland DH 110, an initial production order for the all-weather Sea Vixen interceptor fighter was placed in 1955, as a replacement for the Sea Venom.

Two versions of the Sea Vixen, the Royal Navy's first swept-wing two-seat all-weather fighter, have been produced. The initial production version, the FAW1, first flew in 1957 and was armed with Firestreak air-to-air missiles, Bullpup air-to-surface missiles, guns, rockets and bombs. The FAW2 version was basically similar to the FAW1 and apart from some changes of equipment could carry Red Top air-to-air missiles in place of Firestreaks. The FAW2 also had deeper tail-booms which extended forward of the wing and can be clearly seen in the photograph.

The Royal Navy's first Sea Vixen Squadron (No.892) was formed in 1959. The FAW2 version of the Sea Vixen began to arrive at RNAS Yeovilton in the summer of 1965 and equipped 766 Squadron, the All-Weather Fighter Training Squadron.

The Sea Vixen carried a pilot and an observer and was powered by two Rolls-Royce Avon turbo-jet engines, which gave the aircraft a maximum speed of 720 mph. It had a length of 53 feet 6 inches and a wingspan of 50 feet.

FR AVIATION LTD

IAL

HENRY COOCH LTD

The Type 42 guided missile destroyer HMS Manchester.

DPR (N) M.o.D.

His Majesty King George V stands by the 15 inch guns of the First World War battleship HMS Queen Elizabeth.

In private collection Lieut-Cdr Maurice Board, RN.

A twin 30mm BMARC Oerlikon anti-aircraft gun in action on HMS Manchester (left).

Navy International Magazine.

GUNS IN THE ROYAL NAVY

From the sixteenth century until the Second World War, the gun was the principal weapon of the Fleet in the Royal Navy.

By the end of the eighteenth century, the smooth-bore muzzle-loading cannon had evolved into an effective although not very accurate weapon, capable of firing a variety of shot designed for different purposes. No real advance in armament design took place in the Royal Navy until after the Crimean War, when the muzzle-loading rifled gun was introduced. By the 1880s, the introduction of slow-burning powder and the need for higher muzzle velocities which required longer gun barrels, resulted in the development of the breech-loading rifled gun, the forerunner of the modern gun. The evolution of the big gun, firing a high explosive shell, transformed the wooden sailing warship into the heavily armoured steel battleship of the late nineteenth century. When the first all big gun battleship HMS *Dreadnought* was constructed in 1905, it made all previous warships obsolete overnight, and the race was on to build bigger and better battleships heavily armed with more and bigger guns. The battleship reached the peak of its development during the First World War, while in the Second World War the battleship was eclipsed by the aircraft carrier as the capital ship. The gun had given way to the aircraft and its weaponry.

RNVR Parade, London, June 12th, 1954.

Associated Newspapers Ltd.

HM The Queen reviews RNVR.

DPR (N) M.o.D.

DPR (N) M.o.D.

THE ROYAL NAVAL RESERVE

The Royal Naval Reserve is a force of volunteers who train, in their spare time, in peace for war tasks to complement the regular strength of the Royal Navy.

In 1853, the Naval Volunteer Act provided for the recall of Naval pensioners and for the retention in the Royal Navy, during emergencies, of men who had completed their engagements. The Royal Naval Reserve (Volunteer) Act passed in 1859 authorised a Reserve of trained merchant seamen. In the year 1905, anxiety about the growing strength of the German Navy led to the Naval Forces Act, which instituted the formation of the Royal Naval Volunteer Reserve, the first Reserve of civilian volunteers. Just before the Second World War, the Royal Naval Volunteer Supplementary Reserve was founded, but since disbanded, and following the end of World War II, the Womens' Royal Naval Reserve was formed in 1951. On 1 November 1958, The RNR and the RNVR were merged to form the Royal Naval Reserve as we know it today.

The RNR is an essential and totally integrated part of the Royal Navy. Those who join, many in their teens or early twenties, are so committed that they willingly give up much of their spare time to train to the high professional standards of the Royal Navy. They train mainly to man the ships of the Royal Navy's minesweeping squadrons at one of the eleven RNR Sea Training centres. Another role assigned to the RNR is Naval Control of Shipping, which involves the organising and control of convoys of merchant vessels in time of war. Men and women train in twelve Communications Training Centres, often inland, to augment the Royal Navy's communications organisation at home and abroad. Deck Officers of the Merchant Navy train to man Ships Taken Up From Trade, such as were used in the Falklands Conflict, and to provide liaison officers between the Merchant Navy and the Royal Navy.

Members of the Royal Naval Reserve have given valuable service on a number of occasions since the end of World War II, such as the Korean and Suez crises and more recently, during the Falklands Conflict.

The London Division of the Royal Naval Reserve has recently taken delivery of HMS *Humber,* fifth of the River Class of Fleet Minesweepers.

In the photograph, HMS *Humber* is seen heading downriver, having passed under Tower Bridge.

HMS *Humber* was built at the Lowestoft yard of Richards (Shipbuilders) Ltd. She was ordered in May 1983, laid down in October of the same year, launched in May 1984 and handed over to the Royal Navy in March 1985.

The River Class Minesweepers are designed to carry out deep water minesweeping operations and also to train Royal Naval Reserve personnel. All but one of the class, HMS *Blackwater* are manned by RNR crews. The 800 tonne vessels are based on the design of North Sea supply vessels and they are provided with accommodation for seven officers and twenty-three ratings.

HAWKER HUNTERS OF THE FLEET AIR ARM

Flying high are Hawker Hunter GA11 aircraft of the Fleet Requirements and Direction Unit (FRADU) based at RNAS Yeovilton. For several years a formation of four aircraft from this unit known as the 'Blue Herons' gave aerobatic displays at airshows throughout the country.

Although almost 2,000 Hawker Hunters were built, very few saw service with the Fleet Air Arm. Some Hunter F4s were converted into GA11 trainers for use by the Royal Navy as single-seat advanced ground attack training aircraft and fitted with arrester hooks. These can be seen in the retracted position in the photograph. A photographic reconnaisance

Richard Wilson.

version of the GA11 with cameras housed in a detachable nose-cone was known as the Hunter PR11.

Another Fleet Air Arm Hunter was the T8. Also fitted with airfield arrester gear for training purposes, this was the Naval version of the T7. The prototype first flew in 1958.

The Hawker Hunter had a length of 48 feet 11 inches, a wingspan of 33 feet 8 inches and was powered by a Rolls-Royce Avon turbo-jet engine. Maximum speed was Mach 0.84, although the Hunter could become supersonic in a shallow dive at height.

LANG BROTHERS LIMITED —
"LANGS SUPREME SCOTCH WHISKY"

Richard Wilson.

BUCCANEER REFUELS PHANTOM

A McDonnell Douglas Phantom FG1 of 892 Squadron is refuelled in flight by a Hawker Siddeley Buccaneer S2 of 809 Squadron. The group photograph shows 809 Squadron at RAF Honington, their shore base. Both photographs were taken in 1974.

Designed for the Royal Navy as a low-level strike aircraft to be operated from aircraft carriers, the Hawker Siddeley (originally Blackburn) Buccaneer first flew in 1958. The Fleet Air Arm's first operational squadron of Buccaneer S1s was commissioned at Lossiemouth in 1962. The following year also at Lossiemouth, No.809 Squadron became the second unit to be equipped with Buccaneers, being responsible for the operational development of the new aircraft, until the completion of the programme in 1965. No.809 Squadron was re-commissioned at Lossiemouth in 1966 with the new Buccaneer S2, which gave an additional 30 per cent increase in thrust over the original mark.

After 1969, most of the Fleet Air Arm's Buccaneers were transferred to the RAF. The first four were delivered to No.12 Squadron based at RAF Honington.

The Buccaneer S2 carried a crew of a pilot and an observer, had a length of 62 feet 5 inches and a wingspan of 42 feet 6 inches. Power was supplied by two Rolls-Royce Spey turbo-jet engines, which gave a maximum speed of 600 knots plus.

A PHANTOM PREPARES FOR TAKE OFF

The McDonnell Douglas Phantom entered operational service with the Royal Navy in 1969 and served aboard the Fleet aircraft carriers HMS *Eagle* and HMS *Ark Royal*. With the paying off of *Eagle* at the beginning of the 'seventies and of *Ark Royal* in 1978, the Royal Navy lost the capability to operate conventional fixed-wing aircraft at sea, although the new class of aircraft carrier now in service operates the versatile STOVL Sea Harrier.

The Phantom was an American built aircraft powered by two British Rolls-Royce Spey turbo-jet engines with re-heat facilities, giving it a maximum speed in excess of Mach 2. This all-weather ground attack fighter aircraft has an impressive range and performance. It was capable of carrying a heavy weapon load including air-to-air missiles, nuclear and conventional weapons. It could also be used for photographic reconnaisance. The Phantom carried a crew of two, had a length of 58 feet and a wingspan of 38 feet. The Royal Navy's Phantom aircraft are now operated by the Royal Air Force.

DPR (N) M.o.D.

HMY *BRITANNIA* AT TOWER BRIDGE

The decision to build the present Royal Yacht, as a replacement for the 50 year old *Victoria and Albert,* which was no longer seaworthy, was announced by the Admiralty in October 1951. Built by John Brown's (Clydebank) Ltd., *Britannia* was laid down in 1952, launched by Her Majesty The Queen in 1953 and completed in 1954.

The Royal Yacht *Britannia* was designed for two purposes. Primarily she serves as an official and private residence for The Queen and other members of the Royal Family, when they are engaged in overseas visits or voyages in home waters. She also has the speed and special facilities to enable her to be converted into a hospital ship in time of war. The Royal Yacht also takes part in some naval exercises and undertakes routine hydrographic tasks while at sea. She has a modern clipper bow and a modified cruiser stern, instead of the traditional swan bow and counter stern of previous Royal Yachts.

Merchant Navy practice was followed in *Britannia's* construction and her structural plans were submitted for approval by both Lloyd's Register of Shipping and the Admiralty. She underwent a major refit in 1972 and 1973 and is shortly to commence another.

Britannia has a length of 125.65 metres, a beam of 16.76 metres and a mean draught of 5.2 metres. Her gross tonnage is 5,862 tonnes and she is capable of a continuous seagoing speed of 21 knots. Denny-Brown single fin stabilisers are fitted, to reduce roll in bad weather from 20 degrees to 6 degrees. Power is provided by geared turbines developing 12,000 shp and driving two shafts. The Royal Apartments are aft on the weatherdecks and staff are accommodated on the lower deck. In her wartime role, the aft part would have wards accommodating up to 200 patients.

The Royal Yacht is an independent command administered personally by the Flag Officer Royal Yachts, who is normally appointed an Extra Equerry to The Queen and as such, is a member of the Royal Household. *Britannia* has a complement of 21 Officers and 256 men, all of whom are volunteers from the Royal Navy. A Royal Marines Band, comprising a Director of Music and 26 Musicians is normally embarked for all major overseas tours. Traditions of dress on board include the wearing, by seamen, of the jumper inside the trousers, which are finished by a black bow at the back. White badges, instead of the customary red, are also worn on blue uniforms. Where possible, orders on the upper deck are executed without spoken words or commands and by long tradition, the customary naval mark of respect of piping the side is paid only to The Queen.

CITY OF LONDON

HMS *ODIN*

During World War II, the 'A' Class design of British submarine then in commission, easily surpassed any other type of naval weapon system in its influence on undersea warfare.

In the late 1950s and early 1960s, two new classes of conventionally powered diesel-electric submarines were introduced; these were the Porpoise and Oberon Classes. They comprised the Patrol section of the submarine Flotilla and represented the more traditional view of life on board a submarine — a small control room, cramped accommodation and periscope continuously moving up and down in a constant bustle of activity.

With the introduction of the nuclear powered Fleet submarine in the mid 1960s, it was thought that the diesel-electric boat might be seen to be outdated and unnecessary, but in actual fact, the SSK, as it is known, is the quietest submarine of them all.

The fit of the 'O' boats, as they are popularly known, is not so sophisticated as their nuclear-powered counterparts. The SSK still has to work out its position with the aid of a sextant, built into the periscope.

The power for submarines of the Porpoise and Oberon Classes is provided by two enormous batteries, each made up of 448 separate 2.5 volt cells. Recharging, by the two huge V 16 diesel generators, has to be done when the submarine is on the surface, or at periscope depth by a process known as 'snorting', when air is drawn in through a snorkel pipe or mast. Their tall streamlined fins enclose the periscopes etc, and the bulbous projection on the bow contains the radar and sonar fit.

Shown in the photograph is an interestingly dramatic view of HMS *Odin*. Commissioned on 3rd May 1962, HMS *Odin* is one of the fifteen submarines of the Porpoise and Oberon Class currently in service and on her 'sail' can clearly be seen the figure of a 'Viking'.

It is planned to replace submarines of the Porpoise and Oberon Classes in the 1990s with a new class of submarine, the Type 2400. The first boat of this new class, HMS *Upholder*, is now under construction and three more have been ordered.

DPR (N) M.o.D.

MARCONI COMMUNICATION SYSTEMS LTD   GRASEBY MARINE, A DIVISION OF GRASEBY DYNAMICS LTD   SPUNALLOYS LIMITED

Richard Wilson.

848 SQUADRON IN BORNEO

Just as RN helicopters had played a big part in the campaign against communist terrorists in Malaya during the 1950s, so Naval helicopters were to play an even more important role during the Malaysian/Indonesian confrontation, flying thousands of sorties over dense jungle to counter the guerilla threat.

After the British Government relinquished sovereignty over North Borneo and Sarawak in 1963, guerillas from Indonesian Borneo made numerous raids across the border and these continued sporadically until 1966, when the confrontation ended.

In 1965, during the confrontation, a detachment from 848 Squadron based on HMS *Albion* was stationed at Nangagaat in Borneo. Operating Wessex HU5 helicopters, the detachment supplied military patrols operating in the jungle against the Indonesian terrorists.

Such was the nature of the dense jungle terrain that without the use of the helicopter, the outcome of the conflict could have been very different.

HARRISONS & CROSFIELD plc

HMS AURORA

. . . HMS *Aurora,* one of the Royal Navy's longest serving Leander Class frigates, celebrated her 21st anniversary in 1985. She was built on the Clyde and entered service in 1964, having since steamed thousands of miles all over the world.

Aurora was designed to carry out a general purpose role in addition to her main anti-submarine capabilities. In 1972, she was converted into a more sophisticated anti-submarine frigate with the installation of an Ikara anti-submarine missile system, which replaced the twin 4.5 inch gun mounted forward. In addition she has a multi-purpose Lynx or Wasp anti-submarine helicopter and is fitted with the Sea Cat anti-aircraft missile system. A triple barrelled anti-submarine mortar is mounted aft. Five other frigates of this class have been converted to Ikara Leanders.

She has a ship's complement of 240 Officers and ratings, which includes specialists from all Branches of the Royal Navy. Importance is attached to welfare facilities. Sick bays are well equipped, dining arrangements are good and a well stocked library is available and films and broadcasts are presented. The *Aurora* is powered by two sets of steam turbines, driving two screws and is fitted with stabilisers.

The first HMS *Aurora* was a captured French frigate, which entered service with the Royal Navy in 1758. The Battle Honours displayed by the present HMS *Aurora,* the ninth ship to bear the name are: St. Lucia 1778, Minorca 1798, Guadelupe 1810, China 1900, Dogger Bank 1915, Norway 1940, Bismark 1941, Malta Convoys 1941, Mediterranean 1941-43, Sicily 1943, Salerno 1943, Aegean 1944. The eighth ship to bear the name was one of the Arethusa Class cruisers; during the Second World War she was called "The Silver Phantom" by the Italians, because she was so effective in leading night raids from Malta in 1941 and 1942. She was disposed of in 1947 and went into service with the Nationalist Chinese Navy in 1948 but soon fell into the hands of the Communists and served with them briefly before being sunk. She was salvaged in 1950 and is reported to have remained afloat as a harbour hulk for several years.

Sea Cat: A close-range anti-aircraft missile. Control is by radar tracking and visual guidance; propulsion is by solid fuel. One of the missile systems fitted on HMS Aurora.

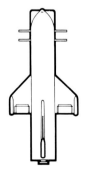

Ikara: A rocket propelled anti-submarine missile designed to deliver homing torpedoes. This is also fitted on HMS Aurora.

DPR (N) M.o.D.

Michael Turner. By kind permission of The Science Museum.

Deck hockey, a popular recreation, on the Flight Deck during a lull in flying operations, November 1970.

C.O.I.

A BUCCANEER LANDS ON THE OLD ARK ROYAL

Ark Royal is one of the proudest and oldest names in the Royal Navy. The first *Ark Royal* served as the flagship of the Lord High Admiral at the time of the Spanish Armada in 1588, although another three centuries passed before another warship was named *Ark Royal*. This First World War vessel became the first to be completed exclusively for seaplane carrier work and began *Ark Royal's* long association with Naval aviation and the Fleet Air Arm, an association which continues today with the present aircraft carrier *Ark Royal*.

The fourth *Ark Royal* was built by Cammell Laird at Birkenhead. Laid down in 1943 during the Second World War, she was not launched until 1950 and entered service in 1955. Built as an armoured Fleet carrier, she was destined to become one of the most famous ships in the Fleet. At the time of the Queen's Silver Jubilee Fleet Review in 1977, *Ark Royal* was the flagship of the Commander-in-Chief and she became a household name through the television series *"Sailor"*, which was filmed on board.

Ark Royal was the first British carrier to be fitted with steam catapults and operated Buccaneer, Phantom and Gannet aircraft and also Wessex and Sea King helicopters. With a displacement of 43,000 tons, *Ark Royal* was 720 feet in length and carried a complement of 2,570 Officers and men. *Ark Royal* was paid off for the last time in 1978 after having steamed almost one million miles during her illustrious career.

RAYCHEM LTD

FIREFIGHTING

Fire at sea is probably one of the greatest horrors known to man. All members of the Royal Navy are well trained in the techniques of firefighting, fire prevention and rescue both at sea and ashore. Part of every sailor's basic training at HMS *Raleigh* includes instruction and practice in basic firefighting and rescue and survival techniques. There is a special unit devoted to this aspect of training.

The principal Royal Navy Firefighting School is located at HMS *Phoenix*, near Portsmouth. This establishment is devoted to specialist training in naval firefighting and rescue and has the latest equipment and simulator facilities. At the time of the catastrophic Mexican earthquake a small team of specialists from HMS *Phoenix* was sent to Mexico City. They were equipped with the latest heat-seeking cameras, to enable them to assist in the location of some of the buried victims.

Every Naval Air Station has its own fully equipped firefighting team which is always on standby when aircraft are flying. Naval Airmen (Aircraft Handlers) are specially trained at the Firefighting School at the School of Aircraft Handling in HMS *Seahawk* at the Royal Naval Air Station at Culdrose in Cornwall. Here they learn particular techniques of rescue from a crashed aircraft and how to fight and control an aircraft fire.

    RICHARD DUNSTON (HESSLE) LTD   THE WALTER KIDDE COMPANY LTD   LLOYD'S REGISTER OF SHIPPING

DPR (N) M.o.D.

HMS *TAMAR* — HONG KONG

The photograph shows HMS *Tamar,* the British Naval Base in Hong Kong. Hong Kong has been a free port since 1842 and a British Naval presence has existed there since 1846.

The present HMS *Tamar,* one of the Royal Navy's foremost overseas shore establishments, was completed in 1979. In keeping with its neighbours, it is a skyscraper style building, which now forms a prominent feature of the Hong Kong harbour scene.

Among the Royal Navy units based at HMS *Tamar* is the Hong Kong Squadron. This is comprised of five, purpose-built, fast patrol craft of the Peacock Class. These are HMS *Peacock* (P239), HMS *Plover* (P240), HMS *Starling* (P241), HMS *Swallow* (P242) and HMS *Swift* (P243). These vessels have a displacement of 716 tonnes and carry an armament of a 76mm gun and close range weapons. They each carry a crew of 31 and have the ability to stay at sea during typhoons.

The role of the Squadron is to assist with the maintenance of Hong Kong's stability and the integrity of its territorial waters. Consequently it co-operates very closely with The Royal Hong Kong Police, the Immigration Department and the Marine and Customs & Excise Departments in combating the Port's major problems of drug smuggling, illegal immigration and modern day piracy. The Hong Kong Squadron also provides an Ocean-going Search and Rescue capability and is equipped to help in the recovery of aircraft or vessels in distress.

JOHN SWIRE & SONS LIMITED   **THE CHINA NAVIGATION COMPANY LIMITED**   **SCOTTS' OF GREENOCK (Est. 1711) LIMITED**   85

DPR (N) M.o.D.

DPR (N) M.o.D.

Operation Christmas Pudding. Admiral Sir John Fieldhouse — Chief of Defence Staff, and Lady Fieldhouse — adding a generous 'tot' of Pusser's Rum, when they assisted with the traditional mixing of the Christmas pudding at HMS *St. Vincent.*

A RE-ENACTMENT OF A 19th CENTURY RUM ISSUE

For over 300 years, the Royal Navy dispensed a rum issue. It was first introduced in 1655 on the West Indies Station at Jamaica, as an alternative to beer, which did not keep or travel well. By 1731, it was in general use throughout the Fleet, as a palliative to poor food and living conditions. The rum ration was then two gills (½ pint) of neat rum a day, divided into two issues, one between the hours of 10 and 12 in the forenoon and the other between 4 and 6 in the afternoon.

At first, the practice was to drink the rum neat, in drams, but this was seen to have many ill effects to both health and morals. It was, therefore, ordered that the rum be mixed in the proportion of a quart of water to every half pint of rum. This was to be done on deck, in a scuttled butt especially kept for that purpose, in the presence of the lieutenant of the Watch, who's task it was to see that the men were not defrauded of their fair share.

The originator of this practice was Admiral Sir Edward Vernon, who, on account of the grogram material of the waterproof boat cloak he wore, was nicknamed *"Old Grogram"*. The rum and water mixture had to have a name and with the seaman's traditional inventiveness, the word *"grog"* was coined and thus entered the sailor's vocabulary.

The story of rum in the Royal Navy is largely that of the social changes which took place in England and in life at sea from the middle of the 17th Century until the mid 20th Century. From 1650 and throughout the 18th Century, shipboard life on the lower deck was incredibly hard and the rum issue played a large part in reducing sensitivity and making life bearable. Operational requirements were very different in the old time Navy. The mental alertness required for packing a cannonball into a muzzle loader was very different to that required to operate a modern electronically controlled weapons system or gas-turbine engine.

Because of this, the rum issue was finally abolished on 31st July 1970, by the command of the then First Sea Lord, Admiral of the Fleet Sir Michael Le Fanu and the Admiralty Board.

The reason for the abolition was simply that the men functioned more efficiently without it and in a highly technical environment, no risk of error, which might be attributed to the effects of rum, could be allowed.

So it was, on 1st August 1970, known as *"Black Tot Day"*, the tradition ceased. All around the world, glasses were raised in their final salute — "The Queen" they said, with many a tear at the passing of such an old and fine tradition.

Although the long history of a rum issue in the Royal Navy ended on "Black Tot Day", an afterglow helps to keep the tradition alive in the minds of seamen. In 1970, The Admiralty donated the sum of £2.7 million, by way of compensation for the abolition of the rum ration. This was considered to be the amount of money which would have been used for the purchase of one year's supply of rum. This money was used to establish the Sailors Fund. This fund, often called the 'Tot Fund', has been operating successfully for more than a decade, under a committee representing the various naval commands. Already it has disbursed considerable sums of money on capital costs for the improvement of living conditions and amenities in general both at sea and ashore.

MORGAN FURZE & CO LTD   PUSSER'S RUM LTD

THE HAWKER HARRIER DEMONSTRATES ITS CAPABILITY

As part of an exhibition of naval equipment on show to the delegates who attended the Atlantic Treaty Association Seminar which was held at The Royal Naval College, Greenwich in June 1975, a Hawker Siddley Harrier Aircraft, which was then being developed for service with the Royal Navy, was on show in HMS *Fearless* (Captain J. B. Rumble RN) which was berthed near the College.

The aircraft, flown by Mr. J. Farley, Hawker Siddley's test pilot, landed on the deck of HMS *Fearless,* as she approached the College on the day before the Seminar. Its unusual flying capability was demonstrated when it flew off, almost vertically into the sky, from the flight deck of HMS *Fearless,* on the last day. This memorable moment was captured by the camera and can be seen in our photograph.

The Royal Navy was aware of the potential of this aircraft at sea, from the earliest days and in 1975 ordered 24 Maritime Harriers to be built, with a revised navigation/attack system and a new forward-looking radar. It was then re-named *"The Sea Harrier"* and in 1978 an additional order for a further ten of these aircraft was made. On 21st August 1978 the first production Sea Harrier made its initial flight and the first deck landing was made on HMS *Hermes.* In 1979, the 700A Naval Air Squadron, the first Sea Harrier Squadron, commissioned and in the next year, 800 Naval Air Squadron was the first 'front line' Sea Harrier Squadron to commission.

INCO ENGINEERED PRODUCTS LIMITED

DPR (N) M.o.D.

HMS *PHOEBE*

HMS *Phoebe* was built on the Clyde and was commissioned in 1966. She was originally based at Chatham, but deployed world-wide visiting many overseas ports including the Far East, the Middle East, West Indies and United States.

HMS *Phoebe* is an Exocet Leander Class Frigate of approximately 2,590 tonnes displacement. The Leander Class was the largest class of frigates to be built for the Royal Navy since World War II. Originally armed with a 4.5 inch gun, they have all been given major refits to accommodate missile armament. They are now divided into three main types, the *Ikara,* the *Exocet* and the *Seawolf* Leanders. The *Exocet* Leander type, to which HMS *Phoebe* belongs is an anti-surface strike frigate, though with her Lynx helicopter embarked she retains a very strong anti-submarine capability.

In 1973, HMS *Phoebe* became a TV star as the first "HMS *Hero*" in the BBC Television series "Warship". Other ships subsequently took the part, but they have all used HMS *Phoebe's* pennant number 'F 42' for their TV role.

In 1974 HMS *Phoebe* began her long Exocet conversion refit in Devonport and in January 1984 completed her latest conversion to Towed Array Sonar. She is currently a fully operational member of the Seventh Frigate Squadron.

Exocet being fired.

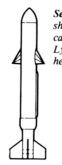

Sea Skua: *An anti-surface ship missile; which is carried by HMS* **Phoebe's** *Lynx multi-purpose helicopter.*

Exocet: *A medium-range surface-to-surface missile with a very low trajectory and a radar homing head as carried on HMS* **Phoebe** *and destroyers.*

THORN EMI ELECTRONICS LIMITED

HMS BRONINGTON (M 1115)

HMS *Bronington* is one of the Coniston Class of mine countermeasures vessels, all named after villages in the United Kingdom who's names end in the letters 'TON'. These ships were originally built as minesweepers, but many have been converted to minehunters. Minehunters have wire sweeps to counter the buoyant mines, but their primary task is to hunt for and safely explode mines on the seabed, using sonar and remotely controlled equipment. They are of a wood and aluminium non-magnetic construction and displace some 420 tons. They have a length of 46.6 metres, a beam of 8.8 metres and are powered by powerful Deltic diesel engines. All the vessels have modern communications and computerised navigation equipment and a 40mm gun gives them a secondary role as patrol vessels. The crew of each ship comprises five officers and thirty-four men.

HMS *Bronington* was built by Messrs Cook, Welton and Grammel Ltd (now Drypool Ltd) at Beverley, just north of the River Humber. She was completed in 1954 and takes her name from a small village in Clwyd, N. Wales. For the first four years of her life, she was named HMS *Humber* and served as a sea-going tender for the RNVR. In 1958 she commissioned for the first time as HMS *Bronington* and began her Royal Navy career, joining the Minesweeping Squadron in the Firth of Forth. She had a major refit at Rosyth in 1964, converting her to a coastal minehunter and in 1966, she joined the First Mine Countermeasures Squadron. In January 1974 she had a second major refit in Gibraltar and returned to home waters early in 1975.

HMS *Bronington* might never have achieved public attention, but for the fact that early in 1976 the then Lieutenant, The Prince of Wales, RN, was appointed her Commanding Officer — a great tribute to this splendid class of ship.

*In our photographs, HMS **Bronington** is seen moored in the Pool of London, with the Tower clearly visible in the background. It was during this visit, in November 1976, that HM The Queen, together with HRH Prince Philip, visited their eldest son on board his ship.*

*As a minehunter, HMS **Bronington** has taken part in a number of crashed aircraft recoveries, a task for which she is particularly suited. In April 1977, the ship commenced a further four-month refit at Rosyth after which she rejoined the First Mine Countermeasures Squadron, operating principally in the Irish Sea, the Firth of Forth, the Clyde and the North Sea. HMS **Bronington** is now serving with the Second Mine Countermeasures Squadron.*

DPR (N) M.o.D.

NATIONAL WESTMINSTER BANK

T.R.H. Highness Duke and Duchess of York's wedding cake. DPR (N) M.o.D.

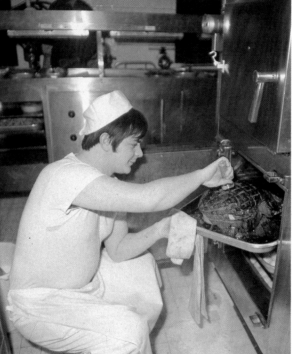

CATERING IN THE ROYAL NAVY

In the 17th and 18th Centuries, the food provided for the sailors on board Royal Navy ships was so poor, maggot-ridden, and uneatable, and conditions generally so hard, that the rum ration was introduced as a palliative. Today, things are very different indeed and the daily menus on a nuclear powered submarine often include such delicacies as steaks and scampi.

With more than 60,000 men and women to feed, serving in Royal Navy ships and shore establishments both at home and abroad, the work of the Catering Section of the Supply and Secretariat Branch is of the utmost importance. The standard of food is especially good; it has to be because of its tremendous bearing upon the morale of men at sea. The choice is good and the food is always plentiful, varied and nutritious.

Royal Navy cooks work hard and are well appreciated. They have the advantages of the latest in catering equipment and techniques and receive a first class training. Until the closure of the Chatham Naval Base in 1984, Royal Navy Cooks, Stewards and Caterers were trained at the Royal Navy Supply School in HMS *Pembroke.* Today, the Supply School is located in HMS *Raleigh,* alongside the New Entry Training Establishment, at Torpoint in Cornwall. All Royal Navy Cooks receive part of their training there and part at the Royal Navy School of Cookery at Aldershot.

In addition to the Cooks and Caterers, important work is carried out by the Stewards. Stewards are responsible for the day-to-day running of the Officers' Wardrooms, both ashore and afloat. Their duties include the serving of food and drink and the upkeep of accommodation. WRNS

Stewards are employed in shore establishments and the picture shows a WRNS Steward serving at table.

As well as being proficient in their everyday skills, Royal Navy Cooks are also experts in all forms of specialist and decorative cookery, from preparing a full formal banquet, to the highly specialised culinary art of cake baking and decorating. Also shown on this page is the commissioning cake for HMS *Ark Royal,* about to be ceremonially cut in the presence of Her Majesty the Queen Mother. Royal Navy Cooks have been honoured with the responsibility of making the wedding cakes for their Royal Highnesses the Prince and Princess of Wales and more recently for the marriage of HRH Prince Andrew to Miss Sarah Ferguson, now their Royal Highnesses the Duke and Duchess of York.

DPR (N) M.o.D.

RFA 'OLNA' REFUELLING A FRIGATE AT SEA

RFA *Olna* is one of three Fleet Tankers which entered service in 1955-66 especially equipped for fuel replenishment at sea. These vessels which displace approximately 18,897 tonnes are fitted with sophisticated machinery and equipment systems and have a helicopter landing platform located aft.

The Royal Fleet Auxiliary is a mainly civilian manned fleet, owned and operated by the Ministry of Defence. Its main tasks are to supply warships of the Royal Navy with fuel, food, stores and ammunition so as to keep them operational whilst away from their bases. It also provides sea transport for Army units and their equipment when required. The ships of the RFA are similar to their counterparts used in commercial work, but are fitted with special equipment to enable them to replenish warships whilst under way. During fuel replenishment, the two vessels, linked by flexible hoses maintain a steady course, at the same time ensuring freedom to manoeuvre in hostile conditions. This modern technique is performed by no other branch of the Merchant Service. The transfer of stores is similarly carried out by Jackstay rigs. The Royal Navy has a world-wide role and RFA ships accompany Royal Navy warships wherever they may go.

The Royal Fleet Auxiliary Service originated in the days of coal-burning ships and was officially constituted by Royal Charter in 1911. At first it was mainly a coal-bunkering and store carrying service, but as oil burning warships replaced coal burners before and during World War I, it was adapted to the new need by the building of a tanker fleet. It grew rapidly and during World War II RFA ships served in every theatre of naval operations from the Arctic to the Pacific, when warships often operated and fought at great distances from their bases. The RFA played a vital part in important convoy operations such as those to Malta and Murmansk. RFA officers and men distinguished themselves and many were decorated.

Since those days, the RFA has played an equally important role with the Royal Navy off Korea, Suez, Cyprus, in the Mozambique Channel, Kuwait, Borneo, Belize, Aden, the Gulf of Oman and of course during the South Atlantic Campaign in 1982. It was during this conflict that the Logistic Landing Ship, *Sir Galahad,* was so tragically lost with heavy casualties whilst preparing to land two Companies of the Welsh Guards with their equipment at Fitzroy Settlement on Wednesday, 9 June. At the same time, her sister ship *Sir Tristram* was badly damaged.

Even more recently, RFA *Brambleleaf* supporting HMY *Britannia,* assisted with the evacuation of British and foreign nationals from South Yemen when Civil War suddenly erupted there.

The Royal Fleet Auxiliary currently comprises a fleet of some thirty ships which include large Fleet Tankers, Replenishment Ships, Helicopter Support Ships, and Logistic Landing Ships.

DPR (N) M.o.D.

RFA tanker refuels Type 42.

ESSO PETROLEUM COMPANY LTD.

DPR (N) M.o.D.

WASP LANDS ON NORTH SEA OIL RIG

The Royal Navy carries out regular surveillance patrols of the offshore gas and oilfield installations in the North Sea. It is also responsible for the protection of our fishing grounds around the British Isles. Both these duties are carried out by the Navy's Fishery Protection Squadron.

Developed from the Westland Scout, the Wasp light helicopter was designed primarily to operate from frigates and destroyers in the anti-submarine role, carrying either torpedoes or guided missiles. Wasps have also been used for search and rescue, training and surveillance duties. The first Naval Wasp helicopter flew in 1962 and in 1963 extensive trials were conducted on the frigate HMS *Nubian,* when more than 200 landings were made.

The Wasp is now only carried by a few Leander and Rothesay Class frigates and will be replaced by the Lynx. The Wasp carries a pilot and is powered by a Rolls-Royce Nimbus gas-turbine engine. It has a length of 40 feet 4 inches, a rotor diameter of 32 feet 3 inches and a maximum speed of 120 mph.

A sea of winches. The PCT Group plc (incorporating Coubro & Scrutton Limited) has a long history of supply and service to H.M. Forces, the Merchant Navy and shipping, ports and harbours throughout the World. More recently this has extended to include major oil and gas exploration and production projects off-shore.

COUBRO NATIONAL LIFTING

WESSEX HELICOPTERS OVER St MICHAEL'S MOUNT

The Westland Wessex first entered service with the Royal Navy in 1961 and after a quarter of a century it still fulfills a useful role today.

Three marks of this versatile helicopter were built for Naval service. The Wessex Mk 1 was a single-engined gas-turbine powered helicopter designed primarily for the anti-submarine role. It could carry homing torpedoes, air-to-surface missiles or rockets. A Royal Marines Commando assault version of the Mk 1 entered service in 1962. During the winter of 1966/67 the Wessex Mk 3 with advanced radar and sonar equipment entered service as a replacement for the Mk 1. Initially the Mk 1 remained operational in the search and rescue role.

The Wessex Mk 5 was an all-purpose twin-engined helicopter which entered service in 1964. It was originally used in the troop carrying role by the Royal Marines Commando. Bulky loads could be slung underneath for rapid transit and air-to-ground missiles, guns or rockets could also be carried. The Wessex Mk 5 is still in service today, performing an invaluable service in the search and rescue role.

Depending on the Wessex's role, one or two pilots were carried, with an aircrewman and diver for search and rescue operations, or an observer and sonar operator in the anti-submarine role. Wessex helicopters had a length of 65 feet 9 inches, a rotor diameter of 56 feet and a maximum speed of 120 mph.

DPR (N) M.o.D.

DPR (N) M.o.D.

WHIRLWIND OVER SALISBURY CATHEDRAL

American-built Whirlwinds equipped the Royal Navy's first operational helicopter squadron in 1952 and a year later saw action in Malaya for the first time. Equipped with dipping sonar gear, Whirlwinds also became the Royal Navy's first anti-submarine unit, commencing operational duties in 1954. The British-built Westland Whirlwind prototype for the Navy first flew in 1953.

In addition to their early anti-submarine role, Whirlwinds were used extensively for search and rescue operations, becoming a familiar sight around our coasts. The Whirlwind was also carried by the ice patrol ship HMS *Endurance*, before being replaced by Wasp and more recently, Lynx helicopters. Whirlwinds were withdrawn from service in the Royal Navy during the late 1970s. They were powered by a Rolls-Royce Gnome turbine engine and carried a pilot, aircrewman and diver with facilities to carry six to eight persons. Whirlwinds had a length of 62 feet 4 inches, a rotor diameter of 53 feet and a maximum speed of 104 mph.

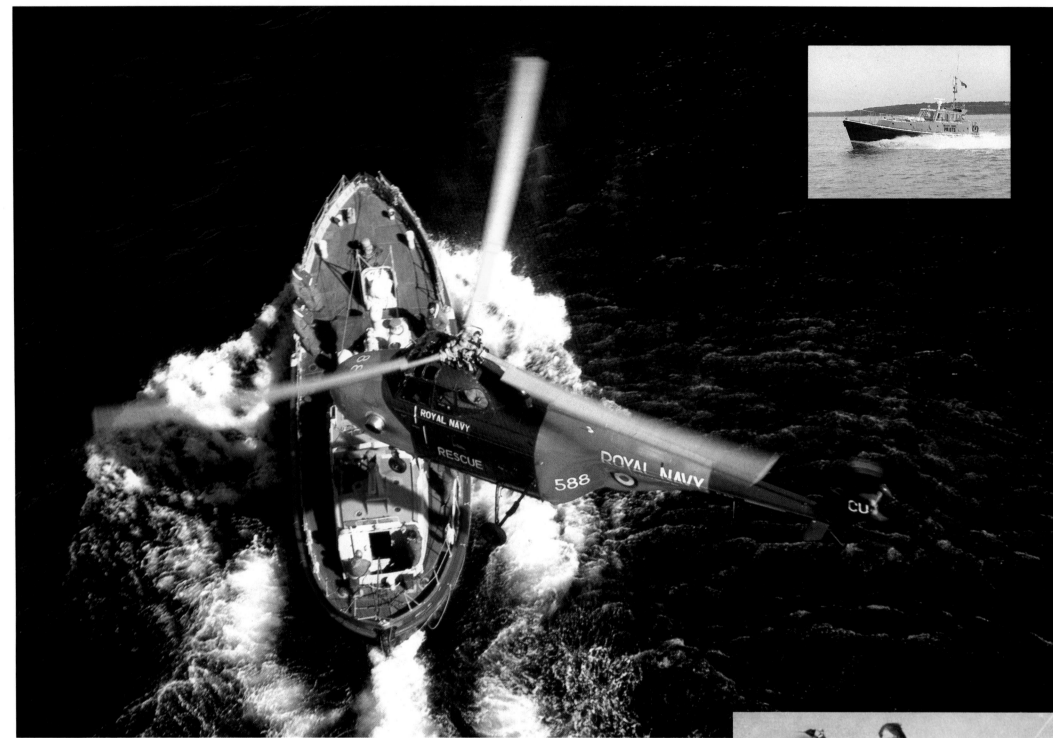

Richard Wilson.

WHIRLWIND SEARCH AND RESCUE

Search and rescue is the most important non-combat activity of the helicopter in the Royal Navy. Naval helicopters form part of a national search and rescue organisation which covers the whole of the British Isles and is responsible for the locating and rescue of anyone in distress at sea or around the coast.

When Whirlwinds entered service in 1952, they equipped the Royal Navy's first operational helicopter squadron and Whirlwinds also equipped the Navy's first helicopter anti-submarine unit, commencing operational duties in 1954. In addition to a crew consisting of a pilot, aircrewman and diver, the Westland Whirlwind could carry up to eight other persons, especially useful in the search and rescue role. Whirlwinds were also used for ice patrol ship duties in the Antarctic.

TRINITY HOUSE PILOT LAUNCH *(ABOVE)*

The *Nelson 44* Pilot Launch, manufactured by Halmatic Limited of Havant, Hampshire, is a development of its predecessor, the well proven *Nelson 40*, in service at many Trinity House ports. It is of the semi-displacement type, giving exceptional seaworthiness and an ability to operate under virtually all conditions.

The new design has increased flare to the forward sections and a greater beam-to-length ratio, both of which combine to give a much drier ride, yet retaining all the other attributes of the original design.

The Atlantic 21 was designed in the 1960s by Rear Admiral D. J. Hoare, CB, MIMechE, MRINA, provost of the United College of the Atlantic in South Wales from which the craft obtains her name. He developed the craft in conjunction with the RNLI who subsequently adopted it for service in 1972. Constant refinements stimulated by experience gained from craft in active service with the RNLI, the North Sea Oil Industry and International Lifeboat Services have produced the most tested, reliable, responsive and seaworthy craft of its type anywhere in the world.

HALMATIC LTD   OSBORNE RESCUE BOATS LTD

DPR (N) M.o.D.

FISHERY PROTECTION

Members of a boarding party from the Island Class Patrol Vessel HMS *Anglesey* (1059 tonnes) on a routine visit to the fishing trawler *'Valiant'*.

Testing the gauge of trawling nets being used and ensuring that internationally agreed rules and regulations regarding fishing on the high seas are observed, is part of the tasks carried out by the Royal Navy's Fishery Protection Squadron. They are also responsible for safeguarding the interests and safety of British fishing vessels going about their lawful business in home waters. Their duties include the patrolling of Britain's offshore gas and oilfield installations.

The Royal Navy's Fishery Protection Squadron consists of a Coastal and Offshore Division. The Coastal Division comprises seven 'Ton Class' mine countermeasures vessels and patrol boats, employed on fishery protection duties off the coasts of the British Isles. The 'Island Class' patrol vessels, of which HMS *Anglesey* is one, form the Offshore Division, which in addition to their fishery protection tasks outside of the 12 mile coastal limit, carry out regular surveillance patrols of the offshore gas and oilfield installations. The first of a new class of offshore patrol vessels HMS *Leeds Castle* (1550 tonnes) was launched in 1980.

THE PORPOISE CLASS SUBMARINE — HMS *WALRUS*

HMS *Walrus* was built at The Greenock yard of Scott's Shipbuilding and Engineering Co. and entered service in 1961. She was one of the eight Porpoise Class submarines, the forerunners of the Oberon Class, which were accepted into the Royal Navy between 1958 and 1961. HMS *Walrus* and HMS *Sealion* are the only two of this class still in service and have been modernised.

The Porpoise Class submarines displace 1,605 tons standard and 2,405 tons submerged. They are 95 feet long and have eight 21 inch torpedo tubes; six in the bow and two in the stern. They are powered by two diesel-electric sets, each driven by an Admiralty Standard Range 16 cylinder diesel engine. Electric motors drive the two shafts, giving a speed of more than

15 knots when submerged. The batteries which power the electric motors are recharged by diesel generators and to reduce the possibility of detection, the air for the diesel engine can be drawn in down the Snort system, while the submarine remains submerged.

Oxygen replenishment and carbon-monoxide elimination make it possible for the submarine to remain submerged without the use of the Snort system for several days and distilling equipment produces fresh water from the sea. The ability to remain submerged for several weeks; the high underwater speed; well proved and efficient control systems and the most up-to-date sonar (underwater detection equipment) make these submarines formidable adversaries.

Porpoise Class submarines are fitted with high definition radar, principally for use as an aid to navigation in poor visibility. They are also fitted with interception equipment to detect searching radar pulses from enemy ships and aircraft. The Porpoise Class submarines are also armed with homing torpedoes and have a large reload capacity. The living conditions are of the highest standard with air conditioning for either Artic or tropical waters. They are complemented by six officers and 65 men.

The other submarines of this class which are no longer in service were — HMS *Cachalot, Finwhale, Grampus, Norwhale, Porpoise* and *Rorqual.*

ENGELHARD LIMITED   THE LINGARD GROUP including MEDISCUS PRODUCTS LTD   ROTHMANS INTERNATIONAL

Type 42 destroyer HMS Southampton fires one of her Sea Dart air-defence missiles. The ship's primary role is to provide air defence for task group operations. She also carries the multi-purpose high speed Lynx helicopter, armed with anti-submarine weapons and anti-ship missiles.

NAVAL MISSILES

Guided missiles are now the principal weapons used in today's Royal Navy and range from the large nuclear deterrent ballistic Polaris missile to the small Seacat anti-aircraft missile.

The Polaris missile is fitted with a nuclear warhead and has a range of 2,500 nautical miles. Sixteen are carried in each of the four Polaris type submarines, which were especially built for these missiles. The Trident II (D-5) missile system will replace this missile system in the future programme for the UK contribution to the NATO strategic nuclear deterrent. The Sub-Harpoon long range anti-ship missile is the principal anti-surface ship weapon in the Fleet type nuclear-powered submarines. The Mk.24 Tigerfish torpedo, one of the most advanced acoustic homing torpedos in the world is carried in the Patrol type submarines. The Exocet medium-range anti-ship missile is carried in the Type 22 Broadsword Class, Amazon and twelve of the Leander Class frigates and in the County Class destroyers, which also have the Seaslug ship-to-air missile. The close range anti-aircraft and anti-missile missile Sea Wolf is fitted in the Broadsword Class and some Leander Class frigates. The Sea Dart medium-range ship-to-air missile with an anti-ship capability is in the Invincible Class aircraft carriers and Type 42 destroyers. The long range anti-submarine missile Ikara is carried in seven Leander Class frigates and the Seacat close-range anti-aircraft missile is fitted in many frigates, destroyers and the Assault ships. The Harpoon surface-to-surface anti-ship low-level-trajectory missile will be fitted in the latest Type 22 and the new Type 23 Class frigates.

The Sidewinder air-to-air guided missile and the Sea Eagle long-range sea skimming anti-ship missile are carried in the Sea Harrier aircraft. The Sea Skua anti-surface missiles are carried by the Lynx multi-purpose helicopter and the AS 12 air-to-surface missile is used by the Wasp and Wessex helicopters, mainly as an anti-patrol boat missile. The SS 11, an anti-tank missile, is used by Wessex helicopters, in support of the Royal Marines Commandos.

The new Sting Ray advanced lightweight torpedo can be launched from fixed-wing aircraft, helicopters and surface ships. Its speed, manoeuvrability and deep diving capability and the ability to operate in shallow water, enable the torpedo to engage a wide range of targets. The Mk.44 and Mk.46 anti-submarine homing torpedos can be dropped by helicopter or fired from surface ships. Deck-mounted tubes for these are fitted in the Broadsword, Amazon, Leander Class frigates and Type 42 and County Class destroyers.

A Seacat missile being launched.

DPR (N) M.o.D.

HMS INVINCIBLE

HMS *Invincible* (RO5) is the first of the new class of modern aircraft carriers to be taken into service by the Royal Navy. She was built by Vickers Shipbuilders Limited at Barrow-in-Furness and was the largest warship to be laid down for the Royal Navy since the 1950s. She was launched by Her Majesty, The Queen in May 1977, entered service in 1980 and played a vital role in the South Atlantic Falklands Campaign in 1982.

The primary function of HMS *Invincible* and her sister ships HMS *Illustrious* and HMS *Ark Royal* is to provide facilities for the command and control of maritime forces; to deploy Sea King anti-submarine and airborne early warning helicopters in support of a force at sea and to provide air defence using Sea Harrier aircraft and the Sea Dart missile system. In addition, the Sea Dart system can be used against surface targets and the Sea Harriers against surface and land targets. A Ski Jump launching ramp is fitted at the forward end of the flight deck. This was invented by Lieutenant Commander D. Taylor, RN, an Engineer Officer. He showed that by launching the Sea Harrier on an upward trajectory, considerable performance gains were achieved, compared with the traditional flat deck launch. Like any ship of her size and type, HMS *Invincible* has a considerable capability to assist in civil emergencies in peacetime.

Invincible has a ship's complement of almost 1,000 Officers and Ratings from all branches of the Royal Navy. The air-conditioned accommodation and catering facilities are of the highest standard and comfortable recreation spaces are provided which are separate from the sleeping areas. The sick bay is equipped to deal with practically any medical emergency and the dental surgery contains the very latest equipment.

The ship is 210 metres long overall, has a maximum beam of 35 metres and displaces around 17,000 tonnes. The hangar below the flight deck is served by two aircraft lifts and the whole ship incorporates the very latest arrangements for operation and survival in the hostile environments of radiation, nuclear fall-out and chemical warfare. She is powered by four Rolls-Royce Olympus Gas Turbines, from the same family as those fitted to Concorde. The engines drive two shafts through the largest reversing gearboxes installed in any ship in the Western World. Designed and built by David Brown Limited, these gearboxes allow any number of engines to be coupled-in, according to the speed required. Electrical power, sufficient to light a small town, is provided by eight Paxman Valenta Diesel Generators (similar to those used in the High Speed train). Large distilling plants make fresh water for domestic use. Stabilisers, automatic steering gear and direct control of the main engines from the bridge are among the many modern features of the ship.

The present HMS *Invincible* is the sixth ship of the Royal Navy to bear the name. The first was the French 74-gun *"L'Invincible"*, captured off Finisterre in 1747. The second was a third-rate 74-gun ship built at Deptford in 1765 and the third also of the same class was built at Woolwich. The fourth was an armour plated "broadside" ship, mounting 14 guns which saw action in the Egyptian war in 1882. The fifth was a battlecruiser which in the First World War saw action off Heligoland and at the Battle of the Falkland Islands in 1914, before being lost at Jutland in 1916.

The Battle Honours carried by the present HMS *Invincible* are: St. Vincent 1780, Chesapeake 1781, St. Kitts 1782, Glorious First of June 1794, Trinidad 1787, Alexandria 1882, Heligoland 1914, Falkland Islands 1914, Jutland 1916 and Falkland Islands 1982.

*Vickers' Barrow-in-Furness Yard — **Invincible** at an advanced stage on her building berth. Note the opening for the aircraft lift to the hanger.*

DPR (N) M.o.D.

*HM The Queen launches **Invincible**.*

On trials.

**VICKERS SHIPBUILDING &
ENGINEERING LIMITED**

Modern Radar systems are the eyes and ears of the Navy. Trained operators use them to provide immediate information about the movements of ships, submarines and aircraft. The picture shows a WRNS Radar Operator, working alongside a Naval Officer, interpreting the information that is appearing on the radar screen.

A WRNS Motor Transport Driver affixes the Admiral's flag to the official car, before embarking her VIP passenger. WRNS MT Drivers' duties have also included driving light lorries and vans as well as cars and the work has involved transporting stores and driving passengers on official visits to and around establishments. These duties are now to be taken over, mainly by MoD civilian drivers.

A WRNS photographer takes an aerial shot from a Naval helicopter. Photography has many uses in the Royal Navy, from ceremonial occasions to training films and pictures. WRNS Photographers help to provide a shore-based photographic service for the Royal Navy and Royal Marines and their work covers cine, video and still photography.

A WRNS Meteorological Observer at work on the preparation of a weather chart. Weather affects all aspects of Naval sea and air operations and is a very real consideration when tactical decisions are being taken. Accurate forecasts are vital to ships, submarines and Naval aircraft and the WRNS Meteorological Observer helps with the information that goes into each forecast.

Her Royal Highness, The Princess Anne, in her uniform as Chief Commandant of the Women's Royal Naval Service.

DPR (N) M.o.D.

THE WOMEN'S ROYAL NAVAL SERVICE

Following their disbanding in 1919, after the end of World War I, many ex-WRNS kept in touch through the Association of Wrens and a magazine "The Wren", edited by Miss Vera Laughton.

In April 1939, with war clouds once more gathering, the WRNS was re-formed and Mrs Vera Laughton Mathews (she had married since World War I and was later to become a Dame) was appointed Director of the Women's Royal Naval Service. She held this important post right through the war until November 1946.

The duties undertaken by WRNS personnel in World War II were even greater than those performed in the first World War. By 1944 numbers reached a peak of 74,635 members, serving in 90 rating categories and 50 Officer branches. Admiral Sir William James, GCB, a former Chief of Naval Intelligence, summed up their achievements in this way — "It is impossible to overstate the value of the service given by the WRNS. Without them it would have been impossible to conduct the Naval War". That value was officially recognised on 1st February 1949 when the Director WRNS of that time, Dame Jocelyn Woollcombe, succeeded in getting the Women's Royal Naval Service recognised as an integral part of the Naval Service.

Today, WRNS serve in all key areas of the Naval Organisation; at Command Headquarters, Naval Bases and Naval Air Stations; at Royal Marines depots and training establishments; with the Ministry of Defence in London and at NATO Headquarters and with Naval Detachments abroad. They do not usually go to sea, but in every other respect they make an equal contribution sharing many of the same jobs and responsibilities, using the same skills and working together with their Royal Navy and Royal Marines counterparts. Appointments for WRNS Officers range from communications, personnel selection and supply work to engineering, computer programming, weapon practice evaluation and meteorology.

Chief Commandant of the Women's Royal Naval Service is Her Royal Highness, Princess Anne.

*Distant ahead: USS **Richard E. Bird**; rear: Canadian ship **Skeena**, following Soviet aircraft carrier **Kiev**.*

Marines storm a beach.

DPR (N) M.o.D.

NATO SHIPS ON PATROL

The North Atlantic Treaty was signed on 4th April 1949 to counter the fear of further Westward expansion by the Soviet Union. The signing of the Treaty gave birth to a unique alliance to which 16 independent Nations subscribed. They were Belgium, Canada, Denmark, France, Federal Republic of Germany, Greece, Iceland, Italy, Luxembourg, Netherlands, Norway, Portugal, Spain, Turkey, the United Kingdom and the United States.

NATO has played a vital role in the preservation of peace in Europe and the safeguarding of the freedom of its member Nations for more than a third of a century. The policy of the Alliance is to effect the safeguarding of peace by maintaining a sufficient strength of naval, military and air forces to deter aggression. At the same time a readiness to negotiate reductions in forces and armaments and create a more constructive relationship between East and West is actively pursued. The three elements on which NATO policy is based are a creditable deterrence; real disarmament; and genuine detente.

NATO's military organisation is headed by a Military Council, which gives advice and guidance to the three major NATO Commanders of the Alliance. These are the Supreme Allied Commander Europe (SACEUR), The Supreme Allied Commander Atlantic (SACLANT) and the Commander-in-Chief Channel (CINCHAN). These Commanders are responsible for ensuring the effectiveness of NATO forces in their respective Commands. Generally, the forces of member Countries remain under their own national command in peacetime. However, the Standing Naval Force Atlantic (STANFORLANT) and the Standing Naval Force Channel (STANAVFORCHAN) are permanent naval forces of ships, drawn from NATO navies, which operate under the respective NATO Commanders. NATO also maintains a naval on-call force in the Mediterranean.

British naval forces declared to NATO include Polaris submarines, Fleet and Patrol submarines, Aircraft Carriers, Assault Ships, Destroyers and Frigates, Offshore patrol vessels, Mine Countermeasures vessels and Naval aircraft. The Royal Navy's role is to assist with the defence of the home base, to keep open the Polaris submarine deployment routes, to counter the mining threat to the approaches to the European re-inforcement ports, to defend reinforcement and supply shipping and to protect offshore resources.

NATO naval exercises are held on a regular basis and are inevitably monitored by Soviet naval forces. NATO ships are also to be found shadowing their Soviet counterparts, whilst they are engaged on their own exercises.

ICL DEFENCE SYSTEMS

National Maritime Museum, Greenwich.

THE FIRST *ARK ROYAL* (1586-1636)

The first *Ark Royal* was built at the Royal Dockyard at Deptford. Initially, the ship was built for Sir Walter Raleigh, who intended to use her for his project for the colonisation of North America. The ship was to have been called *"Ark Raleigh"*, in accordance with the custom whereby a ship was given a two-part name, with the owner's name forming the second part.

The Crown purchased the ship for £5,000 and the 692 ton, 38 gun ship was renamed *Ark Royal*. It became the flagship of the Lord High Admiral, Lord Howard of Effingham, who led the English Fleet against the Spanish Armada in 1588. In 1596, *Ark Royal* again served as Howard's flagship in the attack on Cadiz.

The accession of James I, in 1603, marked the beginning of a decline in British maritime influence and the ship, which had fallen into disrepair, was reconstructed with an increased tonnage of 800 tons. She was renamed *"Anne Royal"*. However, she saw little further service and was finally broken up at Blackwall, after having run aground in the Thames.

THE LAUNCHING OF HMS *ARK ROYAL*

The first section of the hull of the fifth ship to bear the name *Ark Royal* was laid at the Wallsend Yard of Swan Hunter Shipbuilders Limited on 9th December 1978. Prefabricated sections were moved into position on the berth and over the next 18 months, the ship gradually took shape.

Thousands of the Swan Hunter workforce were proudly involved in the ship's build and by the middle of 1981, the hull was complete and most of the masts and superstructures were in place.

On 2nd January 1981, the ship was ceremoniously launched by Her Majesty Queen Elizabeth, the Queen Mother, who had also launched her immediate predecessor to the undeniable delight of thousands of assembled Tynesiders.

It is of interest to note that, as well as her origins on Tyneside, HMS *Ark Royal* has a strong association with the City of Leeds. Such was the affection of the citizens of Leeds for the fourth *Ark Royal* that they contributed the sum of nine million pounds towards her building and that ship was granted the freedom of the City in 1973. The Lord Mayor and the City of Leeds were delighted to witness the launching of the new *Ark Royal* and to renew their links with a proud naval tradition.

DPR (N) M.o.D.

MACTAGGART, SCOTT & CO LTD

HMS *ARK ROYAL* (1955-1979)

The fourth *Ark Royal* was originally ordered in March 1942, as a 31,600 ton armoured Fleet Carrier, initially the name 'Irresistable' was considered, but it was never approved. When the new carrier was finally commissioned in 1955, after a lengthy re-design and modification period, it was as the 43,060 ton *Ark Royal*. The ship was the first to feature the new British developments of the angled flightdeck, the steam catapult and the mirror landing sight. The Air Group consisted of 40 aircraft, weighing up to 26 tons with recovery speeds of over 135 knots.

The first major refit in 1958-59 saw the introduction of the Scimitar and Sea Vixen aircraft and in 1962, her aircraft were used for local patrols in the Malacca Straits, during the Indonesian confrontations. During a brief visit Home in 1963, a P1127 STOVL aircraft, a predecessor to the Sea Harrier, landed on board for the first time.

A second major refit in 1967-70 saw the extension of the port deck edge and the installation of an amidships catapult which allowed the ship to operate Phantoms as well as Buccaneers and Gannets. From 1970 onwards, *Ark Royal* operated in the Mediterranean, Atlantic and Caribbean, and was adopted by the City of Leeds. The ship achieved popular acclaim through the BBC Television series ''Sailor'' and in the Fleet Review to mark the Queen's Silver Jubilee, *Ark Royal* was the Commander-in-Chief's Flagship. In 1979 *Ark Royal* was paid off and broken up, despite determined efforts to save her.

THE BUILDING OF HMS *ARK ROYAL*

The completed *Ark Royal* is seen, moving slowly and with great dignity, down the River Tyne at the commencement of her journey from Swan Hunter Shipbuilders Yard at Wallsend, to Portsmouth, for her Commissioning Ceremony. Towed by tugs, the contractor's Red Ensign still flies proudly from her stern mast for the last time, prior to being replaced by the White Ensign of the Royal Navy.

DPR (N) M.o.D.

SEA HARRIER ODDS SIX-TO-ONE

Air superiority was a cornerstone of the whole South Atlantic Campaign and since its Sea Harriers were outnumbered by at least six-to-one and it had no land based support, the odds were heavily against the Fleet Air Arm from the outset.

That the Fleet Air Arm managed to achieve this vital air superiority is attributable primarily to the skill and effort of the men who flew and maintained the aircraft and to the quality of the aircraft themselves.

With fewer aircraft available than the Argentinians, it was vital that the Fleet Air Arm's Sea Harriers and helicopters should be air-worthy and flying at all times. In total, 171 Sea Harriers and naval helicopters were deployed in fifteen squadrons.

The Sea Harriers flew 2,000 operational sorties and destroyed 23 enemy aircraft in air-to-air combat. Twenty-eight of the Royal Navy's total of 32 Sea Harriers were deployed during the campaign and only two were lost to enemy ground fire: none were lost in air combat. Royal Navy helicopters flew round the clock, in all weathers.

Although the Sea Harriers were outnumbered by six-to-one, they were more than a match for the men and machines of the Argentinian Air Force. Unused to flying over sea, which makes an aircraft much more vulnerable to radar detection, the Argentinian pilots were inexperienced in this type of combat.

In terms of avionic equipment, the enemy had nothing to rival the head-up display, weapons-aiming sights fitted to the Sea Harriers. Similarly, the Sea Harriers were equipped with an advanced version of the Sidewinder Missile, the AIM 9L, which has a guidance system sensitive enough to be fired from any aspect, unlike the earlier version employed by the Argentinians.

One of the greatest advantages of the Sea Harrier over a conventional fixed-wing aircraft is its ability to 'jump' — both from the ground and in mid-air. This astonishing manoeuvre, known as 'viffing' (vectoring in forward flight) is achieved by turning the four jet nozzles or 'puffer ducts' downwards. By this means, the pilot is able to decelerate and then change direction within seconds. It is an agility which enables the Sea Harrier to turn the tables on any known conventional fighter aircraft in a combat situation.

HAWKER SIDDELEY GROUP plc

SEA KING LANDS — THE 'BATSMAN'

The introduction of the 'batsman' was an inter-war development in the aircraft carrier deck landing technique. Around 1937-38, the Deck-Landing-Control-Officer, more popularly known as the "Batsman", was introduced. Equipped with what appeared to be a pair of oversized table-tennis bats, this officer occupied a position towards the port-side, after-end of the flight deck and controlled the approach of an aircraft landing-on, by a series of mandatory signals indicating either "You are too high — go lower", "Your approach is too fast — go slower", "You are port wing low — correct your attitude", "Your hook is not down", etc, until the final and well-known decisive crossing of the bats, indicating "Cut engine".

The introduction of the 'batsman' was not popular to begin with, since aircraft pilots, who are apt to be independent beings, felt that they did not want to entrust anyone else but themselves in the delicate business of a flight deck landing but, nevertheless, the 'batsman' became an established figure of life aboard an aircraft carrier.

During World War II, good 'batsmen' became trusted figures and some of them developed a highly recognisable style of 'batting'. Also, bearing in mind the responsibility involved in batting a squadron of aircraft on board with the carrier deck pitching like a violent see-saw in mountainous seas, some 'batsmen' developed temperaments akin to the conductor of a symphony orchestra!

'Batsmen' still operate on board aircraft carriers today, controlling the manoeuvring of both helicopter and fixed wing aircraft, before take off and after landing. At nighttime, this task is assisted by the use of more sophisticated illuminated batons in place of the 'bats' used during the daytime.

DPR (N) M.o.D.

LOUIS NEWMARK

DPR (N) M.o.D.

HMS ENDURANCE

HMS *Endurance* is the Royal Navy's Ice Patrol Ship. She supports British interests in Antarctic waters and assists the British Antarctic Survey in carrying out its scientific research programmes. She is fitted with the latest oceanographic and hydrographic surveying equipment, since the Antarctic waters are still largely uncharted and much work remains to be done.

Since commissioning in 1968, HMS *Endurance* has deployed to the Falklands and the Antarctic every year. Her proposed withdrawal from this task, as part of the 1981 Defence Review, is thought to have been of important influence in the Argentine decision to invade the Falkland Islands. *Endurance* participated fully in the Falklands conflict and was involved from the outset of the campaign to the eventual victory. In 1982,

HMS *Endurance* was awarded a Wilkinson Sword of Peace for — "A longstanding and continuing service on behalf of those who live in the Falkland Islands, their Dependencies and South Georgia".

The ship was originally the Danish vessel, *Anita Dan* and is specially constructed for operation in ice. She was converted for Naval purposes in 1968 by Harland and Wolff, Belfast and this work included the installation of scientific and surveying equipment and a flight deck and hangar for two Wasp helicopters. Her red hull and mast is unusual for a Royal Navy ship, but is of great practical use, making her easy to identify in ice, especially from the air. Her buff coloured funnel is in the traditional livery of the Royal Navy's surveying fleet. When operating in ice, the ship can be

controlled from the crow's nest, giving a better view of any channels. Her Wasp helicopters can also assist by locating open routes well ahead of the ship.

HMS *Endurance* has a ship's company of 16 officers and 115 ratings, which includes a small detachment of Royal Marines. She displaces some 4,000 tons, has an overall length of 305 feet (92.9 metres) with a beam of 46 feet (14 metres). The main engine is a Burmeister & Wain 550 VTBF diesel driving a single shaft; this gives a speed of 13 knots and a range of about 12,000 miles.

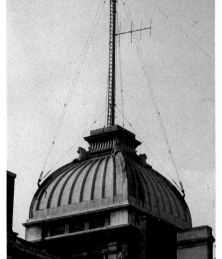

relay a message from London to Portsmouth in twelve minutes.

The use of the Morse Code was introduced into the Royal Navy in 1867. This was entirely due to the perseverance of Vice Admiral Colomb, who succeeded in getting its use accepted in spite of great opposition and its total condemnation at its first sea trials. Its use as a method of maritime signalling has been more than vindicated in the ensuing years. However, until the development of radio, there was never a totally fast and reliable method of conveying essential information more than a short distance.

Today, the need for continuous, accurate and rapid communication between surface ships, submarines and naval aircraft of the Fleet and with Command headquarters and other services ashore is of the utmost importance. The satisfactory Command and control of every aspect of modern naval operations depends on good communications.

To achieve this, the Royal Navy employs many methods, from the continued use of the traditional flashing light, to the most modern techniques employing computer technology and satellite communication links. The above photograph shows the communications centre of a modern Type-42 destroyer.

NAVAL COMMUNICATIONS

Speedy and accurate communication between individual ships of the Fleet and shore bases has always been considered an important aspect of naval operations. For centuries, flag signals were the traditional method of communication in the Royal Navy. The number of flags in use in the naval code comprising what is called a "set" is 58, and consist of 26 alphabetical flags, 10 numeral flags, 16 pendants and 6 special flags. The flags which constitute a signal are termed a "hoist" and one or more hoists can be made at the same time. Hoisted flag signals were later supplemented with the introduction of the use of semaphore as a faster and more flexible method of visual communication. For long range signalling, a semaphore apparatus with arms 9ft to 12ft long was used. This was mounted at the top of the mast and was capable of being trained in the required direction. In Nelson's day, it was possible, by employing the use of a relay of long-range semaphore signals, sited at prominent points such as church towers, to

CS *IRIS*

CS *Iris* is one of three cableships operated by Marine Services Division of British Telecom International at Southampton, to maintain some 18,000 miles of submarine cable around the UK and across the Atlantic.

CS *Iris* was designed, and commissioned in 1976, as a repair ship primarily for use in European waters, but she has demonstrated a world-wide capability for repair and cable laying operations in both shallow and deep water.

The robust and reliable seagoing qualities of CS *Iris* were recognised in her selection for duties as a supply vessel with the Task Force in the South Atlantic, during the Falklands Campaign. One of the longest serving civilian ships, she was subsequently awarded Battle Honours and her Captain and Chief Steward decorated with the OBE and BEM respectively.

SOUTH ATLANTIC TASK FORCE

Among scenes of patriotic emotion that Britain had not witnessed since World War II, the Task Force gathered and set sail for the South Atlantic. The aircraft carriers, HMS *Hermes,* HMS *Invincible* and the assault ship *Fearless* were the first to leave Portsmouth on 5 April 1982. The liner Canberra, carrying Royal Marines and part of the Parachute Regiment followed from Southampton on Good Friday 9 April and the Norland and the QE2 carrying the Guards and the Gurkhas left Southampton on 12 May. In all a modern day armada of over 100 ships including great liners and Hull trawlers, British Rail ferries, cargo ships and the most lethal modern warships sailed south to liberate the Falkland Islands from the Argentine invaders.

The artist Robert Taylor has captured the feeling of the moment in this dramatic marine picture, which never fails to draw comment and discussion. It shows (from left to right) in the background HMS *Glamorgan* a County Class destroyer, HMS *Ardent,* a Type 21 Frigate, the Fleet Auxiliary Tanker RFA *Olna* and the Fleet Replenishment Ship RFA *Resource.* In the foreground are shown HMS *Arrow,* a Type 21 Frigate with her Wasp helicopter, HMS *Hermes,* the flagship of the Task Force Commander, Rear Admiral 'Sandy' Woodward, with Sea King helicopters and Sea Harrier aircraft, and HMS *Sheffield* a Type 42 Destroyer. Of the ships illustrated, two, HMS *Sheffield* and HMS *Ardent,* were fated not to return.

DAVID BROWN GEAR INDUSTRIES LTD

Type of landing made by the Royal Marines on South Georgia.

DPR (N) M.o.D.

GRYTVIKEN — SOUTH GEORGIA

South Georgia is a practically unhabited, mountainous and inhospitable island, some 800 miles south of the Falkland Islands and close to the frozen, forbidding Antarctic Continent. It is British Territory and is administered from Port Stanley. It has a number of derelict whaling stations around its coast and the principal settlement is at the harbour of Grytviken. It was at one of the remote, derelict whaling stations, three bays and 40 miles down from Grytviken, at Leith that the events of 1982 in the South Atlantic first began, when a party of Argentine "scrapmen" arrived to dismantle the old whaling station.

The Royal Navy's ice-patrol ship *Endurance* set out from Port Stanley on Monday 22nd March 1982, with her normal complement of 13 Royal Marines on board, re-inforced by a further 9 from the Royal Marines Company on the Falklands. In command of the Royal Marines Detachment was Lieut. Keith Mills RM, aged 22, his orders were to arrest the Argentine scrapmen and force them to haul down the Argentine flag

that they had hoisted.

They got to Grytviken on Wednesday 24 March and made contact with Steven Martin, commander of the British Antarctic Survey base there, but the Marines were told not to land. Then the crisis deepened and on Wednesday 31 March the Royal Marines landed and *Endurance* left under cover of darkness, and made haste back to the Falklands. On 2 April they heard news of the Falklands Invasion and prepared for an attack. The Argentines moved in force into Grytviken Harbour at 1.040 on 3 April. Lieut. Mills and his Royal Marines succeeded in two hours in shooting down two helicopters and holing the Argentine corvette *Guerrico* before being surrounded by 50 Argentine Marines and forced to surrender. Whilst the invasion was occurring, the members of the British Antarctic Survey team sought shelter in the most solid building in Grytviken — the church. South Georgia and Grytviken were successfully retaken from the Argentinians on 25 April 1982.

CHRISTIAN SALVESEN plc

Michael Turner. By kind permission of The Fleet Air Arm Museum.

SEA HARRIER TAKES OFF FROM HMS *INVINCIBLE*

This dramatic painting shows a Sea Harrier aircraft taking off from the 'ski-jump' flight deck ramp of HMS *Invincible,* while she ploughs through the stormy seas of the South Atlantic during her passage to the Falkland Islands in April 1982. It is of interest to note that, whilst on passage southwards, the livery of the Sea Harrier was changed to an all over grey paint, since this was considered preferable to the white underbelly, which afforded a too distinct visibility.

The Falklands Task Force was centred on the two aircraft carriers HMS *Hermes* and HMS *Invincible.* HMS *Hermes* had a displacement of approximately 25,000 tonnes, with a 220 metre flight deck, fitted with a 12 degree 'ski-jump' launching ramp and HMS *Invincible* displaces approximately 16,500 tonnes and has a 150 metre flight deck, fitted with a 7 degree 'ski-jump' launching ramp.

In peacetime, both aircraft carriers normally carry an aircraft complement of five Sea Harriers and ten Sea King helicopters. The Sea Harriers are primarily used for air-interception, anti-surface ship operations and reconnaisance and the Sea Kings for anti-submarine warfare.

However, for the South Atlantic Campaign, HMS *Hermes* and HMS *Invincible* both took twelve Sea Harriers and fifteen helicopters. On board *Invincible* were the Sea Harriers of 801 Squadron and the Sea Kings of 820 Squadron Fleet Air Arm.

HMS *Invincible* arrived off the Falklands on 1st May 1982 and her Sea Harriers immediately carried out attacks on the Port Stanley air strip and on Goose Green. Thereafter, her aircraft were constantly in action in every role. Throughout the campaign, the carriers proved extremely effective and flexible as command ships and provided the flight deck platforms essential to air operations.

LUCAS AEROSPACE LIMITED

Robert Taylor. Private Collection.

THE 'QE 2' — SAILING SOUTH TO WAR

RMS *Queen Elizabeth 2,* the flagship of the Cunard Line, was requisitioned by the Ministry of Defence on 3rd May 1982. At Southampton she was fitted with three essential helicopter landing decks. Nine days later, on 12th May, under the command of her Master, Captain Peter Jackson, she set sail for the South Atlantic. In his words "She was the only ship in the world that could have done the job. If *QE2* had not been used, the war would definitely have been longer".

The task of the *QE2* was to ferry South the 3,300 men of the 5th Infantry Brigade, among them the Scots and Welsh Guards and the Gurkhas. The *QE2* was the "only ship" because she was able to undertake the run down to South Georgia at the remarkably fast non-stop speed of 29 knots.

As the *QE2* passed 50 miles west of Ascension Island, keeping over the horizon to avoid being sighted, helicopters flew out and embarked Major General Jeremy Moore and his 200 Staff, who were going south to take command of the Falklands Land Forces. The great vessel took a zig-zag course southwards, sailing without lights or radar emissions, to avoid detection. The biggest concern was the possibility of a suicide mission by a lone Argentinian submarine.

The *QE2* called in at Freetown, en-route, to refuel and on the evening of 27th May sailed into Grytviken harbour, South Georgia, in darkness and dense fog, to rendezvous with SS *Canberra*. The troops were cross-decked to *Canberra* and *Norland*, who's tasks were to take 5 Brigade to their landing points at Port San Carlos.

The *QE2* returned to Southampton on 11 June, bringing back the survivors from HM Ships *Coventry, Ardent* and *Antelope,* the ships of the gunline in Falkland Sound which had been lost in ensuring the success of the landing operations. *QE2* was handed back to her owners, Cunard, and made ready once more, for her first commercial voyage on 14th August.

The Royal Navy took up from 'Trade' no less than 54 merchant ships of all shapes and sizes, to support the Task Force. At 67,000 tons, displacement, RMS *QE2* was the largest of these vital vessels.

CUNARD LINE LTD.

ARGENTINE SUBMARINE 'SANTA FE' UNDER ATTACK

The dynamic painting by Michael Turner vividly shows all the drama of the first major action of the South Atlantic Campaign involving British Naval forces.

The Argentine submarine *Santa Fe* had been discovered heading towards the Island of South Georgia in a blizzard. It was on Sunday, 25 April, 1982 when the Wessex Mark 3 Helicopter 'Humphrey' of 737 Naval Air Squadron took off from the County Class guided-missile destroyer HMS *Antrim* to attack the *Santa Fe* with depth charges and AS 12 missiles. She was assisted by Wasp helicopters of 829 Squadron from the Ice Patrol Ship HMS *Endurance*, together with another Wasp helicopter of 829 Squadron, flying from the Type 12 Rothesay Class Frigate HMS *Plymouth*.

The attack was successful and the disabled *Sante Fe* was left discharging smoke and diesel fuel. Listing heavily, she limped towards South Georgia and managed to make the shelter of a bay to the north of the island, where she ran aground close to a disused whaling station at Grytviken.

Her crew surrendered, to be followed next day by the remainder of the Argentine forces on South Georgia.

Salvagemen with **Santa Fe** *alongside being towed by United Towing tug* **Yorkshireman** *with HMS* **Endurance** *in the background. This picture was taken by the RN from HMS* **Endurance's** *helicopter in July 1982.*

Michael Turner. By kind permission of The Fleet Air Arm Museum.

IMI YORKSHIRE ALLOYS LIMITED

UNITED TOWING LIMITED

VEGA-CANTLEY INSTRUMENT CO. LIMITED

*HMS **Plymouth** built 1960/61 Type 12. The Rothesay Class anti-submarine frigate has been modernised to operate Wasp helicopters and Seacat missile systems. Other improvements include full air-conditioning, modernised operations room, better communications facilities and an improved gunnery control system. Her sister ships are HMS **Rothesay**, HMS **Yarmouth** and HMS **Rhyl**.*

"Wimpey Seahorse" belongs to Wimpey Marine of Great Yarmouth. In the Falklands, without this kind of help from the Merchant Navy the Navy could not have completed their task.

THE RE-TAKING OF SOUTH GEORGIA

The picture, taken in the Wardroom of the frigate HMS *Plymouth*, shows her Commanding Officer, Captain D. W. Pentreath C.B.E. D.S.O. RN, together with Captain N. Barker C.B.E. F.R.G.S. RN of HMS *Endurance,* accepting the formal surrender of the Argentine forces in South Georgia, from Captain Alfredo Astiz, the Argentine Garrison Commander.

South Georgia is a virtually uninhabited icy island, some 800 miles South of the main Falkland Islands group. It is administered from Port Stanley and was the first territory to be liberated from the invading Argentinians. It was on South Georgia that the troubles in the South Atlantic began, when a group of Argentinian "scrap metal merchants" arrived to dismantle an old whaling station and raised the blue and white Argentine flag over their operations.

"Operation Paraquet", the code name for the retaking of South Georgia, supplied the hoped for results. However, it nearly ended in disaster, due to the cruel Antarctic weather.

On 25th April 1982, following the successful attack on the Argentine submarine "Santa Fe", Major Guy Sheridan, Royal Marines, led detachments of the SAS and SBS, together with men of 'M' Company, 42 Commando, in an attack on the mountain behind the port of Grytviken. At the same time, HMS *Antrim* and HMS *Plymouth* opened up a bombardment with their 4.5 inch guns. The Argentines promptly surrendered and the victory signal was sent to London in the traditional form — "Be pleased to inform Her Majesty that the White Ensign flies alongside the Union Jack at Grytviken, South Georgia. God Save The Queen".

Hull trawlers forming 11 Squadron MCM in minesweeping formation in the South Atlantic during The Falklands campaign. This picture, taken from the squadron commander's ship HMS **Cordella**, shows (left to right): HMS **Junella**, HMS **Farnella**, HMS **Northella** and HMS **Pict**.

HMS **Farnella** demonstrating her ability to cope with heavy seas in the South Atlantic during The Falklands conflict.

RV **Farnella**, carrying the Institute of Oceanographic Sciences' sidescan sonar GLORIA and specially equipped for numerous other ocean research tasks, at the start of a long term charter to the USGS.

The original painting of HMS **Northella** at South Georgia was presented by the vessel's owners J. Marr and Son Limited to 11 Squadron MCM at Rosyth to mark the safe return of their four trawlers by the Royal Navy following their requisition for The Falklands Task Force.

THE MERCHANT NAVY GIVES SUPPORT

Those who were there say this painting, now owned by 11 Squadron MCM at Rosyth, captures perfectly the bleak stillness of South Georgia. It also records one of the key operations of The Falklands Conflict, the transfer of troops from the *QE2* to the ships which took them to San Carlos Bay to establish the vital bridgehead.

The five Hull trawlers requisitioned for the Task Force made history from the outset as the only STUFT ships (ships taken up from trade) to fly the white ensign and be fully manned by Royal Navy crews. HMS *Cordella*, HMS *Farnella*, HMS *Junella*, HMS *Northella* and HMS *Pict* were subsequently awarded full Royal Navy Battle Honours — fully earned in numerous roles in addition to their final task of detecting and clearing mines.

Designed for arduous work in Arctic waters the trawlers were well able to cope with the worst the South Atlantic could produce and proved ideal for special operations all round the islands with the SBS and SAS.

Royal Navy commanders became so attached to these sturdy and reliable

ships that they were reluctant to return them to their owners and have followed their fortunes closely ever since.

Three, *Cordella, Junella* and *Pict,* resumed their fishing careers and it is perhaps an indication of the Royal Navy's regard for this particular design that *Northella,* featured in the Falkland's painting, has subsequently been regularly employed on special charters to the Royal Navy in training and escort roles.

Some ships, however, seem destined for fame and glory and the fifth trawler, *Farnella,* has become one of the most-travelled and most famous scientific research vessels in the world as flagship of the scientific fleet operated by owners J. Marr Limited of Hull.

On charter to the Indian Government *Farnella* has explored the abyssal depths of the Indian Ocean for rich mineral resources and, with British and American scientists, mapped large areas of the Atlantic and Pacific seabeds to learn more about the origins of our world and the hazards and opportunities that lie in the ocean depths — most of them still largely unexplored.

A final £1.5 million conversion at the beginning of 1986 turned *Farnella* into one of the most versatile research vessels afloat and, for the remainder of the 1980s and through into the '90s, she is scheduled to carry out one of the last great explorations left on earth.

That is the sonar mapping of more than a million square miles of seabed, mostly in the Pacific, for the United States government's Geological Survey (USGS). Using a unique British invention called GLORIA (Geological Long Range Inclined Asdic, a highly productive sidescan sonar developed by the Institute of Oceanographic Sciences of Wormley, Surrey, part of the Natural Environment Research Council) *Farnella* will be producing sonographs which provide a "picture" of the seabed akin to an aerial photograph. These "subsea moonscapes" as scientists have dubbed them provide a wealth of valuable information indicating where earthquake inducing faults lie, where it is safe or otherwise to locate structures such as oil rigs and, above all, the areas likely to yield rich mineral resources.

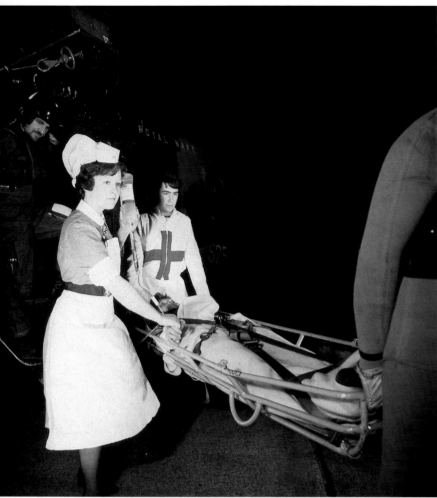

A QARNNS nurse and a Royal Navy Medical Assistant help with the transfer of a casualty from a Wessex Search and Rescue helicopter to a waiting ambulance.

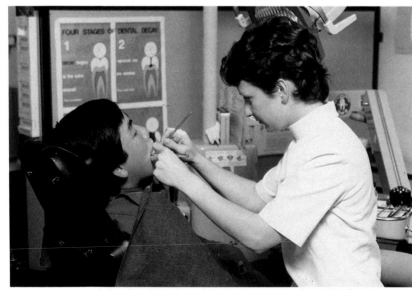

A Leading Wren Dental Hygienist examines the teeth of a young naval rating. Dental Hygienists work under the direction of a Royal Navy Dental Surgeon and have the responsibility of carrying out certain dental treatments, like the scaling and polishing of teeth, to prevent dental disease and disorders of the teeth and gums.

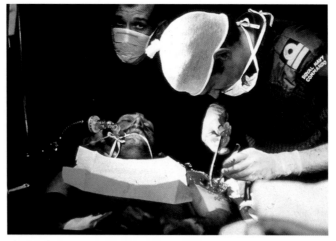

A Royal Navy Surgeon Lieutenant operates on the high-velocity exit wound in the arm of a corporal of the 3rd Parachute Regiment, following the attack on Mt. Longdon during the Falklands Campaign.

Four Surgeons, three aneasthetists and a back-up team of 100 nurses and Medical Assistants worked round the clock, in two improvised operating theatres, in the makeshift hospital which was established in the old meat refrigeration plant at Ajax Bay in East Falklands. 202 major operations were carried out, more than a third of them on Argentine prisoners.

THE ROYAL NAVY MEDICAL BRANCH

The beginnings of Naval Medicine were not very glorious. In Stuart times, when the modern navy dawned, doctors, like most sailors, were pressed into service regardless of age or desire.

Gradually it was realised that the sick and wounded needed to be properly tended and in 1644 Apothecaries and Barber Surgeons eventually co-operated in the choice of 'Sea Surgeons'. Hospitals and hospital ships emerged and surgeons were given crude facilities aboard naval ships. In 1805 the surgeons achieved the status of Officers and naval hospitals were by then established in Portsmouth, Chatham and Plymouth. Towards the end of the ninteenth century the Royal Naval Medical Service was fully established and in 1918 Medical Officers took executive ranks such as Surgeon Captain and adopted the distinguishing red sleeve stripe, denoting their Branch and Profession.

The Naval Nursing Service was established in 1884, when the first trained nurses were appointed to the naval hospitals. Queen Alexandra's Royal Naval Nursing Service was founded in 1902 and today Nursing Officers and Naval Nurses, together with Medical Officers, Medical Assistants and Medical Technicians of the Royal Navy Medical Branch help care for the health and well-being of naval personnel and their families.

In 1983, to conform with the civilian health services, male nursing officers and naval nurses were introduced into QARNNS for the first time.

Left. The picture shows a Wasp Helicopter of 829 Squadron, clearly marked with the Red Cross symbol, winching a casualty down on to the flight deck of HMS **Hydra**, one of the three Survey Ships which were converted for use as Ambulance Ships during the Falklands Campaign.

The ocean going Survey vessels which took part in the transferring of casualties were HMS **Hydra** (A144), HMS **Hecla** (A135) and HMS **Herald** (A138). They worked in close conjunction with the main Hospital Ship SS **Uganda** which was affectionately known as "Mother Hen".

AIRSTRIKE

This dramatic picture was painted by Robert Taylor following a first-hand detailed discussion with the Sea Harrier pilot, Commander 'Sharkey' Ward, DSC AFC RN, who was Commanding Officer of 801 Squadron, Fleet Air Arm, on board HMS *Invincible* throughout the Falklands Campaign. It depicts Commander Ward about to bring down an Argentine Mirage jet on 21 May 1982. The Sea Harrier has just released its Sidewinder missile, which is seen split seconds before destroying the Argentine Mirage. This painting vividly captures the speed and drama of the action and is much admired by all of the Falklands Sea Harrier pilots.

Although the Sea Harriers were outnumbered by six to one, they were more than a match for the men and machines of the *Fuerza Aerea Argentina,* the Argentine Air Force. Unused to flying over sea, the Argentine pilots were inexperienced in this type of combat.

So far as avionic equipment was concerned, the Argentines had nothing to match the head-up display, weapons-aiming sights fitted to the Sea Harriers. In addition, the Sea Harriers were equipped with an advanced version of the Sidewinder missile, the AIM 9L, which has a guidance system sensitive enough to be fired from any position, unlike the earlier version, employed by the Argentinians, which were designed to seek the heat of the target's jet exhaust and thus could only be fired from the astern.

Throughout the Falklands Campaign, the Sea Harriers and the men who flew them more than proved their complete superiority over any other conventional fighter aircraft, in combat.

GEC AVIONICS LIMITED

WELSH GUARDSMEN ARE SAVED FROM THE BURNING *SIR GALAHAD*

At 17.15, on Tuesday 8th June 1982, as the 1st Battalion Welsh Guards were beginning to disembark, two Argentine Skyhawks skimmed low over the inlet near Bluff Cove where the Logistic Landing ships, *Sir Tristram* and *Sir Galahad* were anchored. Both of the ships were hit, *Sir Tristram* the more seriously. Twenty minutes later, at 17.35, there was a second bombing run by a pair of Mirages and an unlucky bomb exploded in the ammunition hold of the *Sir Galahad*. There was a huge explosion aboard followed by a pall of smoke and billowing flame. Immediately, the ship's boats and liferafts were launched and those who could jumped and scrambled over the side and took to the boats. Rescue helicopters approached as close as they could to the stricken ship but, as they worked, waves of heat rose up to meet them and ammunition continued to explode in the blaze, sending bullets whistling in all directions. With extraordinary bravery, the helicopter pilots flew many times back into the cloud of dense smoke, hovering blind, so that their winchmen could pull up survivors. When some of *Sir Galahad's* liferafts drifted back towards the burning ship, the helicopter pilots took their aircraft down almost to sea level, so that the wash from their rotor blades forced the dinghies away again.

The disastrous bombing of *Sir Galahad* and *Sir Tristram* resulted in 55 men being killed and 46 injured, mostly young Welsh Guardsmen. The disaster also effectively destroyed the 1st Ballalion Welsh Guards as a fighting unit, since all of their kit, weapons and ammunition were totally lost. *Sir Galahad* eventually burned out and became a total loss. On 25 June 1982, she was towed out to sea by HMS *Typhoon,* where she was sunk as a war grave.

DPR (N) M.o.D.

BEAUFORT AIR-SEA EQUIPMENT LIMITED

Robert Taylor. In the collection of The Fleet Air Arm Museum.

HRH PRINCE ANDREW ENGAGED IN RESCUE OPERATIONS

The Container Carrier and 'roll-on, roll-off' cargo ship SS *Atlantic Conveyor* was owned by the Cunard Steamship Company. She was built in 1970 and was 18,146 tons, deadweight. At the beginning of the Falklands Campaign, *Atlantic Conveyor* was taken up from Trade by the Ministry of Defence. She was converted at Devonport to operate helicopters and on 25th April 1982, she sailed for the South Atlantic under the command of her Master, Captain I. North DSC. Her cargo comprised vital stores and equipment for the campaign, including Chinook and Wessex helicopters and Sea Harrier aircraft.

A month after she sailed from the UK, on the afternoon of 25th May, the last day of sustained air attack on the Task Force, *Atlantic Conveyor*

together with *Elk* and a Naval escort, started to make a run into San Carlos to off-load her precious cargo. Initially, conditions were ideal, with thick fog effectively masking the operation. Suddenly the fog lifted and the escort decided to turn away; not, however, until the force had been spotted and subjected to a calamitous air attack.

The Argentinian pilots, who saw the *Atlantic Conveyor* only as a large 'blip' on their radar screens, thought she was one of the Task Force's two aircraft carriers and launched a successful attack with Exocet missiles. *Atlantic Conveyor* was hit, set on fire and severely damaged. The loss of her cargo was a savage blow to the Task Force. The three big troop-lifting Chinook helicopters carried by *Conveyor* were to have ferried the British

forces across the island. A fourth Chinook survived, because it was airborne at the time of the attack. The Wessex helicopters which were lost would have flown up artillery and ammunition. Without them, the troops had to walk and the preparations for the final battles took much longer.

Twelve members of the *Atlantic Conveyor's* gallant crew were lost, including her valiant Master. The survivors were rescued from the sea by Royal Navy helicopters and picked up by HMS *Alacrity*. Among the Fleet Air Arm pilots engaged in the rescue operation was HRH Prince Andrew, flying a Sea King helicopter. He is reported to have said that this particular operation was among his most poignant memories of the whole campaign.

DPR (N) M.o.D.

HMS *CHURCHILL* VISITS SAN FRANCISCO

The nuclear-powered Fleet submarine (SSN) HMS *Churchill* is the first of its class and a sister ship of HMS *Conqueror,* the British submarine which sank the *'General Belgrano'*.

Nuclear-powered Fleet submarines are capable of continuous patrols at high under water speed, independent of base support, and can circum-navigate the globe without surfacing. They have three decks and displace 3,556 tonnes. They are armed with wire-guided homing 'Tigerfish' torpedoes.

DPR (N) M.o.D.

THE 'BELGRANO' SINKING

For several days, the Argentine Cruiser *"General Belgrano"*, an old World War II Cruiser of 13,645 tons, had steamed just outside the 200 mile total exclusion zone around the Falklands and crossed into it on at least one occasion, accompanied by her two escort destroyers. Armed with 6-inch and 5-inch guns and fitted with Seacat missiles, she had more fire power than any ship of the British Task Force. During this time she was being shadowed by the nuclear-powered Churchill Class submarine HMS *Conqueror,* under the command of Commander C. L. Wreford-Brown, DSO RN.

The *'Belgrano'* changed course and made towards the Task Force. This information was flashed immediately to Admiral Woodward in his flagship HMS *Hermes*. He in turn, passed it on to Admiral of the Fleet Sir Terence Lewin, Chief of the Defence Staff, who went at once, personally, to the meeting of the War Cabinet at 10 Downing Street and recommended that *Conqueror* should "act to defend the Fleet".

The order went back to HMS *Conqueror* and just before dusk, at 8 p.m. on Sunday, 2 May, 1982, two Tigerfish homing torpedoes were fired at the *'Belgrano'*. They scored a direct hit on the port side and 368 of *'Belgrano's'* 1,100 crew were killed.

The stricken *'Belgrano'* remained afloat for forty minutes before becoming the largest warship to be sunk in a naval action since 1945. The Royal Navy was in no doubt that the correct course of action had been taken, though when the news was announced to the Fleet it was done with a voice of regret.

TECHNITRON LTD   PEGLER-HATTERSLEY plc   CJB DEVELOPMENTS LTD

THE SURRENDER OF WEST FALKLAND

Following the formal surrender at Port Stanley of all of the Argentine forces in the Falkland Islands, General Moore dispatched Lieutenant Colonel Malcolm Hunt, Royal Marines, together with the men of 40 Commando to accept the surrender of the Argentine forces on West Falkland. This was thankfully done without the need of any further fighting, which would have been necessary had not General Menendez ordered the capitulation of all of the Argentine forces on all of the Islands of the group.

Our picture, taken by L.A.(Phot) Alistair Campbell, then serving with 40 Commando, is one of the 'classic' photographs taken at the time. It shows the Union Jack again being raised over West Falkland on 15 June 1982 by Royal Marines of 40 Commando.

This was indeed an appropriate moment, for it was in 1767 that British Marines had first erected a wooden blockhouse at Port Egmont in West Falkland and from 1833 there has been a continuous British presence on the Falkland Islands.

ARGENTINE PRISONER OF WAR

Our picture shows a Lieutenant Commander in the Argentine Marine, who was manning a Forward Observation Post on the high ground above San Carlos. He was captured by Royal Marines of 40 Commando six days after the landings. All the requirements of the Geneva Convention were strictly observed in the handling of Argentine prisoners. It was necessary to blindfold them whilst they were being taken through the British positions, to prevent them from observing anything which might have been useful information, in the unlikely event of their being able to effect an escape.

Following the final surrender, there were 11,000 Argentinian prisoners in Port Stanley alone. The British had no way of coping with such vast numbers, so the Argentine prisoners became in military parlance "self-administering". Other prisoners were brought into Port Stanley in groups. They were set to work for a day clearing up the mess in the town and on the airfield and were then moved to the jetty to be shipped out each evening.

General Menendez and his Senior Staff were taken on board HMS *Fearless,* where they were held until Argentina formally acknowledged defeat.

PROVIDENT MUTUAL LIFE ASSURANCE ASSOCIATION

Invincible returns to a royal welcome.

HMS *INVINCIBLE* RETURNS FROM THE SOUTH ATLANTIC

On 5th April 1982, HMS *Invincible* sailed from Portsmouth carrying Sea Harriers of 801 Squadron and Sea Kings of 820 Squadron. Her Captain was Captain J. J. Black DSO, MBE RN, and among her complement of Sea King pilots was His Royal Highness, Sub-Lieutenant The Prince Andrew. HMS *Invincible* sailed at the head of the Task Force and arrived off the Falklands on 1st May. She remained at sea continuously throughout the campaign, being replenished by ships of the Royal Fleet Auxiliary, her aircraft and helicopters constantly in action.

On 17th September 1982, having been at sea for 166 days, during which time she steamed more than 51,660 miles, she arrived triumphantly back at Portsmouth. On her arrival, she was proudly wearing both the Royal Standard and the flag of the Lord High Admiral, for on board were Her Majesty The Queen and His Royal Highness Prince Philip, Duke of Edinburgh, who had previously been flown on board to greet their son, Prince Andrew, on his safe return.

In the photographs, Her Majesty can be seen receiving a bouquet of flowers on coming ashore with HRH Prince Philip and HRH Prince Andrew, also the Band of the Royal Marines plays, as *Invincible* returns to a tumultuous welcome.

MEL

DPR (N) M.o.D.

HMS HERMES RETURNS FROM THE SOUTH ATLANTIC

In July 1982, HMS *Hermes,* Flagship of the victorious South Atlantic Task Force, made a triumphant return to Portsmouth. She received a tumultuous welcome both ashore and afloat.

With Rear Admiral Sir John Woodward embarked, *Hermes* was the Flagship of the South Atlantic Task Force throughout the Falklands campaign. When *Hermes* sailed from Portsmouth on 5th April 1982, at the beginning of the Falklands crisis, she was carrying almost 2,000 men (her usual complement is 1,421 including aircrew), provisions for 90 days at sea and more than double her normal complement of aircraft. During the conflict, her aircraft operated around the clock and units from the ship destroyed a large number of enemy aircraft in the air and on the ground. By the time HMS *Hermes* returned home she had completed 108 days of unbroken sea service and travelled more than 35,000 miles.

The name *Hermes* has been used by the Royal Navy for over 180 years. The first vessel to bear the name was a captured Dutch merchantman which was renamed *Hermes* in 1796. For the next century six other vessels carried on the tradition. In August 1913 the eighth *Hermes* was converted to a seaplane carrier and effected the first ever flight of an aircraft with folding wings from a ship at sea. The ninth *Hermes,* completed in 1924, was the first ship to be specifically designed by the Admiralty as an aircraft carrier. In 1942 she was attacked and sunk in the Indian Ocean with the loss of 280 lives. The present HMS *Hermes,* a ship of 24,385 tonnes, was launched by Lady Clementine Churchill at Barrow-in-Furness in 1953. Since *Hermes* had a major refit in 1980/81, the most striking visual feature is the 12 degree 'ski-jump' launching ramp fitted on the bows. This enables the Sea Harrier VSTOL aircraft to launch from the flight deck with a much greater load than would otherwise be possible.

RHP GROUP plc

DPR (N) M.o.D.

SS *CANBERRA* RETURNS TO SOUTHAMPTON

The P & O Liner SS *Canberra,* on her arrival back at Southampton after the Falklands Conflict, on 11 July 1982. The rust marks on her hull are visible evidence of the 94 days she had spent continuously at sea, during which time she steamed a total of 25,245 miles.

'Canberra', 44,807 tons gross, was built in 1961 as a luxury cruise liner. On 7 April 1982 she was requisitioned for use as a troopship. As she lay alongside a narrow wharf at Southampton, work instantly began to adapt her for her task. Part of the upper deck fittings were cleared to allow for a helicopter approach to the mid-ships area. The main swimming pool was drained and a structure of steel girders and plates assembled over it to make a helicopter landing pad. The weight of the water in the swimming pool was calculated at 100 tons. The landing pad construction was rapidly but carefully designed to be about the same.

'Canberra' was, in fact, fitted with two helicopter decks and her accommodation modified to carry the troops and provide a casualty clearing station. She embarked 3 Brigade; 40 and 42 Royal Marines Commando, 3rd Battalion Parachute Regiment and associated units. She sailed from Southampton on 9 April under her Captain, D. J. Scott-Masson CBE, with Captain Christopher Burne RN as naval chief and arrived off Ascension Island on 20 April.

On 6 May, *'Canberra'* sailed South to the Falklands. She refuelled at sea several times en-route and entered Falkland Sound on 21 May, loaded with troops for the invasion. That day, she was under air attack for 10 hours, fortunately without sustaining any damage or casualties. On 27 May, the *QE 2* rendezvoused with *'Canberra'* in Grytviken Harbour, South Georgia, where *'Canberra'* embarked 5 Brigade from *QE 2* and then re-entered San Carlos Sound with the troops on 2 June.

'Canberra' was the first major maritime unit to enter Port Stanley Harbour after the surrender. She returned 4,200 Argentine prisoners of war to Puerto Madryn on 19 June and then sailed for Southampton with 3 Brigade on 25 June. Among the British Servicemen, she was known affectionately as "The Great White Whale".

THE PENINSULAR AND ORIENTAL STEAM NAVIGATION COMPANY LIMITED

THE POLARIS SUBMARINE

The Royal Navy's four nuclear-powered Polaris submarines (SSBNs) or 'Bomber Boats' as they are affectionately known, are HMS *Resolution, Renown, Repulse* and *Revenge*. Each carries 16 missiles and they are the United Kingdom's contribution to the Strategic deterrent of the Western Alliance.

Through its association with one single set of circumstances, the word 'deterrent' has become so closely linked with missiles that it has become, for some people, an alternative for 'danger' or 'destruction'. Nothing could be further from the truth. The Polaris deterrent is simply a means of making the use of force by a potential aggressor an unattractive option. It is therefore a keeper of the peace.

It is for this reason that at least one Polaris boat is constantly on patrol and, because of their high speed, long endurance underwater and advanced equipment, they have little fear of detection.

These huge submarines each displace 8,636 tonnes. They are 129.5 metres long and have a beam of 10.1 metres. Three decks provide accommodation which is exceptionally spacious for a submarine and good domestic facilities are available to the crew. An air purification system enables them to remain submerged for a long time without any outside support or need to surface.

Each Polaris submarine has two crews, numbering 147. They are known as the Port and Starboard Crews and when one is away on patrol, the other is training or taking leave.

On board, particularly high priority is given to the quality of food and its importance to morale is recognised by the frequent appearance on the menu of such items as steak and scampi. The essence of life is routine and the avoidance of monotony is treated very seriously. Each week the crew's wives and families are able to send them 40-word messages known as "familygrams" and relaxation is helped by a good supply of current feature films and video TV programmes. Well equipped libraries and study facilities are provided and Polaris submariners have, in fact, been able to obtain Open University degrees, thanks to these.

The Polaris weapon itself is a two-stage ballistic missile, powered by solid fuel rocket motors. It is 9.5 metres long, 1.37 metres in diameter and weighs 2,700 kilos. Fired from the submerged submarine it can devastate a target 2,500 nautical miles away. Polaris submarines also have six conventional torpedo tubes.

FISHER CONTROLS LIMITED   PRECISION SYSTEMS LIMITED   STC DEFENCE SYSTEMS LIMITED

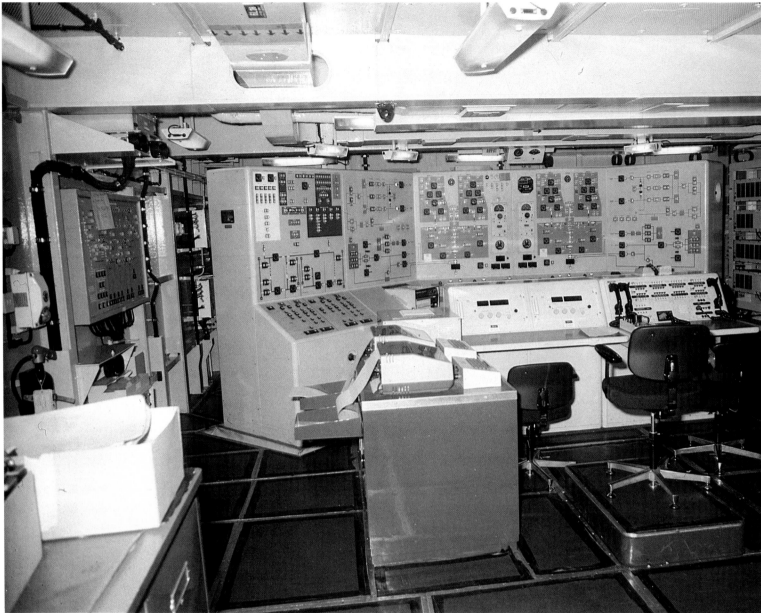

Operations room.

DPR (N) M.o.D.

Chart table.

Hanger.

Stores.

BELOW DECKS IN THE *ARK ROYAL*

The vast aircraft hangar in *Ark Royal* occupies most of the first two decks below the flight deck and is capable of holding all of the aircraft normally carried. To support the variety of complex aircraft, extensive purpose built workshops are housed in compartments located conveniently nearby. The Air Engineering support, which has the capability of carrying out 80% of the complete rebuilding of any aircraft on the ship is provided by some sixty personnel of all the Fleet Air Arm Engineering specialisations.

HMS *Ark Royal* is powered by four Rolls-Royce Olympus Gas Turbines, which are marine versions of the engines that power Concorde and electrical power is provided by 8 Paxman Valenta diesel generators, which produce 12 megawatts. In addition to propulsion and electrical power, there are numerous other services which are required to make the ship habitable and safe. All of these are controlled from the ship's Machinery Control Centre. There are large workshop facilities, where welding, engraving, turning, fitting and many forms of metalwork can be undertaken to maintain the ship's fabric.

Support Services are essential. Stores Accountants maintain and account for 52,000 different items located around the ship or in one of their 14 storerooms. The value of stock held on board is £10,000,000 and the OASIS computer helps keep track on where everything is kept. If an item is held on board it can be located and issued in minutes. The Caterers plan both the menus and the stocks of food held on board. In a normally quiet day, the Cooks have to provide 3,600 meals of a high standard. They also have to be ready to feed the ship's Company at short notice, when the ship is at Action Stations.

If aircraft are to operate safely, it is essential that they have an accurate appreciation of the expected weather conditions. The ship is therefore fitted with modern forecasting equipment, which is operated by meteorological officers and ratings.

These are but a cross section of the essential duties and activities that take place on board the Royal Navy's largest surface ship and are illustrated by the photographs on this page. In all HMS *Ark Royal's* ship's company comprises about 1,100 Officers and men from all Branches of the Royal Navy. Every man has an important job to do, no matter what his specialisation, for the prime ingredient of success in a fighting ship is teamwork.

SMITHS INDUSTRIES AEROSPACE & DEFENCE SYSTEMS LIMITED

DPR (N) M.o.D.

THE BUILDING OF HMS *ARK ROYAL*

When HMS *Ark Royal* arrived in Portsmouth in July 1985, it marked the end of a building programme which had lasted for more than six years and cost some £320,000,000.

The first section of the keel was laid in the Wallsend Yard of Swan Hunter Shipbuilders Limited on 9 December 1978 and over the next eighteen months, prefabricated sections were moved on to the berth and the ship gradually began to take shape.

By mid 1981, the hull was complete and most of the masts and super-structure was in place and on 2 June 1981, the ship was launched by Her Majesty, the Queen Mother. Once safely afloat, the massive task of fitting out the compartments on board was commenced, initially at Wallsend. In September 1982, the ship dry docked for five weeks to install the propellors, rudders and stabilisers. *Ark Royal* emerged from the dock in November and stayed at Wallsend until May 1983, when she moved up river to Walker Yard. In Walker Yard, the ship slowly came alive, machinery began to run, temporary pipes and cables were withdrawn and on 3 May 1984, the main engines were turned for the first time. In July, the ship was dry docked for the second time to allow for the shot blasting of the hull and the application of the necessary special underwater paint. On 19 October 1984, the ship sailed on Contractor's sea trials, which were a resounding success and completed a week ahead of schedule. During the trials, the first Trafalgar Night Dinner was held at sea and the first fifty deck landings completed.

On completion of the Sea Trials, the ship returned to Walker Yard with eight months remaining in which to finish off the 1,400 compartments, and test a multitude of machines, weapons systems, and water, air and power systems. Also to carry out many modifications as a result of lessons learnt from the Falklands Conflict.

A final docking was completed in Hebburn Dock, followed by the Final Machinery Trials period and the operation of the Liquid Oxygen Plant. This was something that had not been possible previously until well after the acceptance of a carrier.

Work toward the final inspection continued to gather pace, with over 1,000 personnel inspecting, cleaning and polishing the ship. On 1 July 1985, Commodore Naval Ship Acceptance and his Staff, inspected the finished ship and declared themselves content and HMS *Ark Royal* joined the Fleet.

DPR (N) M.o.D.

HMS *ARK ROYAL* ACCEPTANCE CEREMONY

The acceptance ceremony of the new HMS *Ark Royal* took place on 1st July 1985. Seen in the photograph is a section of the flight deck, with the ship's company lined up ready for the ceremony to take place. To the right of the picture can be seen some of the civilian workers who participated in the building and between them and the crew are some of the members of the Royal Marines Band, on board for the ceremony.

At the rear of the flight deck can be seen a Sea Harrier STOVL aircraft, together with a World War II Fairey Swordfish of the Fleet Air Arm Historic Flight, based at Yeovilton. This is the type of aircraft that would have flown off the third *Ark Royal* and she was especially flown on board for the acceptance ceremony.

*D86 HMS **Birmingham** prepares to receive her Lynx helicopter on the after flight deck.*

*D92 HMS **Liverpool**, her Sea Dart missiles and 114mm gun at the ready; she is painted in the all-over grey livery, which was introduced during the Falkland Campaign.*

*D88 HMS **Glasgow** turns towards Portland Harbour. Her Lynx helicopter is secured on her flight deck, and the hangar door can be clearly seen.*

*D87 HMS **Newcastle** steams gracefully on a calm sea. Her Sea Dart missile launcher and 114mm automatic rapid-fire gun are clearly visible on the bows and her Lynx helicopter is just visible on the after flight deck.*

DPR (N) M.o.D.

TYPE 42 DESTROYER

The destroyer in the Royal Navy evolved in response to the threat poised by the introduction of the torpedo boat in the 1870s. The Admiralty built a number of torpedo gunboats to counter this threat and these were followed by an enlarged class of vessel which was called a torpedo boat destroyer. This type of ship was fast and manoeuvrable and capable of performing the roles of both torpedo boat and destroyer; it was the forerunner of today's Type 42 destroyers.

The primary role of the Type 42 Class of guided missile destroyer is to provide air defence for task group operations: and two Type 42s, HMS *Sheffield,* the first ship of the class, and her sister ship HMS *Coventry* were lost during the Falklands Campaign, whilst so engaged.

All Type 42 Destroyers are equipped with the Sea Dart medium-range air-defence missile system, which also has an anti-ship capability, the automatic rapid-fire 114mm (4.5 inch) gun and anti-submarine torpedo tubes. They also carry the high speed multi-purpose Lynx helicopter, armed with anti-submarine weapons and the Sea Skua anti-ship missile, which is controlled by the Sea Spray search radar. The latest communications and sensor equipment is fitted in all ships of the Class, which are powered by Rolls-Royce Olympus and Tyne gas turbine engines and fitted with controllable-pitch propellors and stabilisers.

HMS *Birmingham* (D86), *Cardiff* (D108), *Newcastle* (D87) and *Glasgow* (D88) now form Batch 1 of the Class and HMS *Exeter* (D89), *Southampton* (D90), *Nottingham* (D91) and *Liverpool* (D92) form Batch 2. HMS *Manchester* (D95), *Gloucester* (D96), *Edinburgh* (D97) and *York* (D98) *(see page 130),* with an increased length from 125 metres to 139 metres and beam from 14.6 metres to 15.2 metres to provide additional space for future weapon fits, form Batch 3. Batch 1 and 2 ships carry a complement of 280 and Batch 3 ships 297 Officers and men.

HMS Newcastle, built 1978.　　　　　　　　DPR (N) M.o.D.

HMS Liverpool, built 1982.　　　　　　　　DPR (N) M.o.D.

THE LYNX HELICOPTER

The Lynx is an advanced high speed multi-purpose helicopter used by the Royal Navy in an anti-submarine role and for search and strike missions against surface vessels. It entered service with the Navy in 1976. Helicopters play an important role in Naval operations and the Lynx operates from most of the Navy's destroyers and frigates, providing surface surveillance and an anti-submarine warfare capability. The Lynx is the standard fit in Type 42 destroyers and Amazon Class and Broadsword Class frigates. It will initially fit the new Type 23 frigates when they enter service from 1989 onwards.

The Lynx's Seaspray search and tracking radar gives it an over the horizon capability. It can carry the Sea Skua anti-surface ship missile, the Mark 44 homing torpedo and the Sting Ray advanced lightweight torpedo capable of engaging a wide range of targets. The Lynx carries a pilot and observer. It has a length of 14.9 metres, a rotor diameter of 12.8 metres, a speed of 160 knots and is powered by two Rolls-Royce Gem turboshaft engines.

RACAL RADAR DEFENCE SYSTEMS LIMITED　　　　**RACAL AVIONICS LIMITED**　　　　**RACAL ELECTRONICS plc**

HMS *BOXER*

HMS *Boxer* is one of the newest ships to join the Fleet and the eighth Royal Navy ship of that name. She is the first of the Batch 2 'stretched' version of the Broadsword Class, Type 22 frigates. HMS *Boxer* is some 12 metres longer than her predecessors and was built by Yarrow Shipbuilders Limited on the Clyde. She was launched on 17th June 1981 by Lady Pillar, the wife of the then Chief of Fleet Support, Admiral Sir William Pillar, and commissioned on 22nd December 1983 at Plymouth.

The origins of today's missile-carrying frigates go back to the days of sail. The Royal Navy's first frigate was launched in 1757 and in Nelson's time, frigates were known as the eyes of the Fleet. During both of the World Wars, frigates played an important part in sustaining the fight against the German 'U-boat' threat, despite heavy losses. The role of the frigate today has changed little.

HMS *Boxer* is capable of defending herself and attacking targets above, on or below the sea surface. Her weapon fit comprises the Exocet and Sea Wolf missile systems; six anti-submarine torpedo tubes; Lynx anti-submarine helicopters; the Harpoon anti-ship missile and the Goalkeeper close-range gun. Her modern sensors, employing 'state-of-the-art' technology, are designed to provide early and rapid warning of any threat so as to give the command team time to react. HMS *Boxer* is fully air conditioned throughout and the ship is stabilised to optimise weapon and sensor performance, and to provide a more comfortable working platform. *Boxer* is powered by two Rolls-Royce Tyne cruising turbines, which give the ship great endurance and fuel economy and two Rolls-Royce Olympus gas turbines which give the ship an impressive acceleration and top speed.

Equipment supplied by Plessey Naval Systems:

Sonar 2016
STWS II Shipborne Torpedo Weapon System
Sonar 2031 Towed Array
Display Sub Systems for the CACS Command System
RICE II Internal Communications System
Bathythermograph Equipment

HMS *Boxer* has a displacement of 4,800 tonnes with a length of 146.1 metres and a beam of 14.75 metres. She has a draught of 6.4 metres. Her complement numbers 250 Officers and men. Battle Honours include Crimea 1855, Salerno 1943, Sicily 1943 and Anzio 1944.

THE ROYAL MARINES FREE-FALL PARACHUTE TEAM

The Royal Marines free-fall parachute team has existed in its present form since 1977. It is formed from volunteers from within the Corps and provides displays at shows and schools all over the United Kingdom. The team comes under the command of R Company Royal Marines Commando, based at Poole in Dorset, and works closely with the Royal Navy to promote recruiting and favourably project the Navy's public image.

Those men who are nominated for team training spend a year at the Joint Services Parachute Centre at Netheravon, culminating in six weeks winter training in Florida in the United States, during which final selection takes place. Each team member can expect to serve for two years with the display team, before returning to general commando duties.

The team travels to displays in a Royal Navy Wessex Mark 5 helicopter from the Royal Naval Air Station at Yeovilton in Somerset. Crewed by a Pilot and an Aircrewman, the Wessex Mark 5 is powered by two gas turbine engines, has a top speed of 130 miles per hour and is capable of carrying twelve fully armed Commandos or alternatively artillery or vehicles slung underneath. The Wessex has a single sliding door on its starboard side, through which the team makes its exit.

Having determined the wind force and direction, by means of a streamer dropped from the helicopter, the team jump from a height of 10,000 feet. They then display two different kinds of sport parachuting — Relative Work, which is carried out during the free fall, before the parachute is opened, and Canopy Relative Work, displayed after their canopies have opened. Relative Work is the art of free fall. Dropping at speeds of over 120mph, individual team members manoeuvre, changing the attitude of their bodies as they fall and link up to form and display various patterns which are visible from the ground. In Canopy Relative Work, displayed once the canopy has opened, the team members steer their parachutes, so that they can link up in flight to form a pattern or stack, which is controlled by the top man in the formation. The Royal Marines hold a World record with a 22-man stack formed at night and have equalled the World Record with a 23-man day stack as shown in the photograph.

In a subsequent attempt in August 1986, the Royal Marines free-fall parachute team succeeded in creating a new World Record with the formation of a 24-man stack.

Prince Edward, as a new Royal Marine recruit, steers a landing craft on a jungle river.

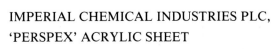

IMPERIAL CHEMICAL INDUSTRIES PLC,

'PERSPEX' ACRYLIC SHEET

John M. A. Farrow, DPR (N).

Robert Taylor. In the collection of Sir Donald Gosling.

DPR (N) M.o.D.

HMS INTREPID — ANTI-NUCLEAR PRE-WETTING

HMS *Intrepid* was built by John Brown & Co (Clydebank) Ltd. in 1965-66 and was first commissioned in March 1967.

Together with her sister ship HMS *Fearless,* she is one of the most versatile craft ever designed for amphibious warfare. She is capable of landing troops of an infantry battalion or Royal Marines Commandoes and their equipment, a squadron of tanks or armoured Scout Cars, or a complete unit of the Royal Engineers with their heavy equipment. As an assault ship she is virtually a streamlined floating dock, surrounded by vehicle stowage space and personnel accommodation. The dock is flooded by taking in sea water ballast to lower the ship in the water.

During amphibious operations, the ship serves as a joint headquarters for Naval and Military Commanders. In the Falklands Conflict, HMS *Intrepid* supported HMS *Fearless,* which served as the flagship of the Commodore in Command of the Amphibious Forces who controlled the whole San Carlos landings and operations in San Carlos Water.

HMS *Intrepid* is 520 feet long, has a beam of 80 feet and displaces 12,000 tons. There are two Seacat missile systems for defence against surface and air attack, together with 20mm, 30mm and 40mm guns. She is powered by two self-contained steam turbines, each driving one shaft. The ship's complement varies with her role. The average is 50 Officers and 500 men, which includes 3 Officers and 85 men of the Royal Marines and a Wessex helicopter detachment of 3 Officers and 19 men of 845 Squadron.

Up to 150 midshipmen can be embarked for nine-week training deployments. HMS *Intrepid,* in the role of Dartmouth Training Ship, provides them with their first Naval sea experience after initial training at Britannia Royal Naval College.

Anti-nuclear pre-wetting is an evolution in which all ship's ports, doors and hatches are fully sealed and decks and surfaces thoroughly washed by powerful high pressure jets of sea water. This is undertaken when the vessel is thought to have been in, or entering, a zone where it is likely to encounter hazard from radioactivity or nuclear fallout.

HMS YORK — D 98 — LATEST TYPE 42

HMS *York* is the latest of the Type 42, Sheffield Class, guided missile Destroyers to be commissioned and she entered service in 1985.

The primary role of this class of guided missile destroyer is to provide air defence for task group operations. They are equipped with the Sea Dart medium-range air-defence missile system, which also has an anti-ship capability and the automatic single-barrel, rapid-fire, 114mm gun, which can be used for self defence anti-aircraft fire, against other ships and for shore bombardment in support of the Army. They are also fitted with two triple anti-submarine torpedo launchers which fire anti-submarine homing torpedoes and give the ship a very rapid offensive anti-submarine capability. Type 42 destroyers also carry the high speed Lynx multi-purpose helicopter armed with anti-submarine weapons and are fitted with the Sea Skua anti-ship missile, which is controlled by the Sea Spray search radar. A Sea Wolf point defence system and BMARC gun are fitted to some ships of the class. HMS *York* is powered by two Rolls-Royce Tyne engines for cruising and two Rolls-Royce Olympus turbines giving a maximum speed exceeding 30 knots, with excellent acceleration. She displaces 3,880 tonnes, is 139 metres long and 15.2 metres in the beam. Her complement is 26 Officers and 275 ratings of all main specialisations.

Because modern warfare requires very quick reaction, all the weapon systems are fully automatic, but the decision to open fire remains with the Captain, who is responsible for the tactical handling and fighting of the ship.

The ship is fitted with a "real time" computer system. With inputs from all sensors, the computers can produce an accurate, up-to-the-minute visual picture, which ensures the effective deployment of weapons. By way of comprehensive and modern communications, including sattelite link, the ship is able to provide information to other ships, aircraft and to the shore.

In a modern complex warship, such as HMS *York,* every man on board has to be an expert in his own field and the emphasis is increasingly placed on technical skills. Creature comforts are not forgotten, though they must, of course, take second place to fighting efficiency.

BONAR BRAY LTD   SERCK HEAT TRANSFER   WOODS OF COLCHESTER LTD INCORP. KEITH BLACKMAN

DPR (N) M.o.D.

ROYAL FLEET AUXILIARY *SIR TRISTRAM*

During the Falklands Conflict in 1982, RFA *Sir Tristram,* a Logistic Landing Ship, under the command of Captain G.R. Green DSC RFA, sailed from Belize via Ascension Island, loaded with troops, stores, three scout helicopters, a 105mm artillery battery and a blowpipe battery. She was the second ship in the line with the assault force, leaving the anchorage just as HMS *Antelope* exploded. She remained with the battle group until 5th June and was only two miles from MV *Atlantic Conveyor* when *Atlantic Conveyor* was hit by an Exocet missile. On 8th June, *Sir Tristram* was bombed and heavily damaged during an attack by Argentine aircraft while she was landing stores and equipment at the Fitzroy Settlement near Bluff Cove. However, she remained afloat and was used as a stores and accommodation ship during the remainder of the campaign. In June 1983, the *Sir Tristram* was put on board the *Dan Lifter* (a heavy lift transporter ship) and brought back to the United Kingdom.

In 1984, the *Sir Tristram* was redesigned and rebuilt. The first phase of the work was to strip out the remains of the aluminium superstructure and replace it with steel. Both the bridge and the radio room were enlarged and the public rooms redesigned in an open plan concept. The after flight deck was enlarged and the overhang reduced saving considerable weight and allowing more light into the cabins below. The vehicle deck was made to double as a fully functional flight deck and is now capable of landing a Chinook helicopter. In addition, the ship was lengthened by 29 feet, the new 120 ton midship section being necessary to support the weight of the new steel accommodation.

The RFA *Sir Tristram,* one of six Logistic Landing Ships built between 1964 and 1967 was built by Hawthorne Leslie at Hebburn-on-Tyne and completed in 1967. Her standard displacement is 6407 tonnes and she is 135 metres in length, with a beam of 18.2 metres. Her normal complement is 65. The Logistic Landing Ships were built to carry heavy stores and equipment and are fitted with bow and stern doors and ramps. They are capable of beach landing and can also operate helicopters. They are normally manned by Royal Fleet Auxiliary Service personnel.

DPR (N) M.o.D.

RFA *SIR TRISTRAM* VISITS THE POOL OF LONDON

On 14th October 1985, after fifteen months of intensive rebuilding at Tyne Ship Repairers Ltd, RFA *Sir Tristram* again with Captain G.R. Green DSC RFA in command, sailed under Tower Bridge and berthed alongside HMS *Belfast* in the Pool of London. The rebuilt ship carried a Sea King helicopter on her after flight deck and a Royal Marines static display on her vehicle deck and made a marvellous sight to those who remembered her from 1982 and her fate in the Falklands Campaign. In fact, it was hard to believe that she was not a completely new vessel.

For the next two days, the ship was open to the general public and hosted visits by schoolchildren and Sea Cadets. On 17th October, 28 Defence Correspondents attended the weekly Defence briefing, which was especially held on board. This allowed the journalists to see for themselves the ship that many thought would not be able to be saved and restored to active service. In the evening of the same day, a fundraising party was held on the ship's tank deck. Contributors to the Lifeboat Fund, personnel who had

served on *Sir Tristram* in 1982 and many personalities from the shipping world were present. The 400 guests donated a very generous sum of £16,755. Captain Gordon Butterworth, President of the RNLI/RFA *Sir Galahad* Lifeboat Fund, presented a cheque for £141,000 to the Deputy Chairman of the RNLI, Vice-Admiral Sir Peter Compston KCB. Following the presentation, a concert of stirring music was presented by the Band of the Royal Marines.

Before her arrival in London, RFA *Sir Tristram* was presented with her Battle Honours by the Director Ships and Fuel, Mr Tony Kemp. In a ceremony held on 2nd October 1985, on the Tyne, Mr Harry Wilson, Production Director of Tyne Ship Repairers, also presented the ship with the encased metal remains of the Purser's safe. Since her return to service, RFA *Sir Tristram* has transported troops to Norway for their Winter exercises and has now returned to her normal LSL duties.

THE ROYAL YACHT RESCUES ENDANGERED BRITONS

In January 1986, HMY *Britannia* was passing southwards through the Red Sea, on passage to Auckland, New Zealand, where she was due to embark Her Majesty The Queen and His Royal Highness The Duke of Edinburgh for a Royal Tour of Australia and New Zealand.

At this time, a fierce civil war, between conflicting Marxist factions, suddenly erupted in the South Yemen and the lives of British and foreign nationals living in that Country, particularly in the port of Aden, were placed in grave danger.

The presence of the Royal Yacht in the vicinity was fortuitous and she was immediately diverted to assist in the evacuation of these unfortunate victims of circumstance.

Due to her conspicuous and easily recognisable unwarlike livery, *Britannia* was able to get quite close inshore, though at one time she nearly came under fire. On the afternoon of 17th January, Rear Admiral Sir John Garnier, Flag Officer Royal Yachts, ordered the ship's boats ashore to pick up evacuees from the beaches. One hundred and thirty evacuees from different countries were taken on board, including about fifty British citizens. They were mainly women and children.

It was the first time in her history that the Royal Yacht had been involved in an evacuation operation under wartime conditions and it is understood that all of her accommodation and facilities, except for the Queen's own personal apartments on board, were adapted to receive the evacuees and

make them comfortable. Even the Royal Marines Band on board played as the evacuees were taken aboard.

Plans for the evacuation were closely co-ordinated between Britain, the Soviet Union and France, who all had interests in the area, and the evacuees were taken by *Britannia* to the safety of Djibouti, where they were disembarked, before *Britannia* continued on her voyage.

Her Majesty The Queen was kept closely informed of developments throughout and was said to have been delighted that the Royal Yacht was able to be put to such good use in assisting in the evacuation.

HMS *SHEFFIELD* — THE PREDECESSOR

HMS *Sheffield* was the first ship of the Class of Type 42 Destroyers, to which she gave her name and was completed in Vickers Yard in 1974.

In our picture, she is seen on a Fleet Exercise in the company of two Royal Navy amphibious Hovercraft.

The primary role of the Type 42 Destroyer is to provide air-defence for task group operations. They are equipped with the Sea Dart air-defence missile system, which also has a good anti-ship capability and an automatic fire 114mm gun and anti-submarine torpedo tubes. They also carry the Lynx helicopter. Powered by Rolls-Royce Olympus and Tyne gas turbine engines, they have controllable pitch propellors. They displace 3,500 tonnes and carry a crew of 280.

After arriving in the South Atlantic, HMS *Sheffield* took up her role of providing anti-aircraft and advance air warning for the aircraft carriers of the Task Force. It was whilst performing this duty on Tuesday 4th May 1982 that she became the first major British casualty of the Falklands Conflict. The attack was made by a low-flying Argentine aircraft, which slipped in below the Fleet's guard. It launched an Exocet air-to-surface missile which hit HMS *Sheffield* amidships, about six feet above the waterline, penetrating directly into her operations centre.

The Exocet missile exploded upwards and outwards, causing extreme damage and killing 20 men and wounding another 24. Within seconds the whole of the working area of the ship was filled with heavy black pungent and acrid smoke, followed by fire. It was the first time that an Exocet missile had been used in anger against a modern warship and its effectiveness was terrible to behold.

After five hours, during which time valiant efforts were made to save the ship and her crew, *Sheffield's* Commanding Officer, Captain J. F. Salt, Royal Navy, reluctantly gave the order to abandon ship. *Sheffield* still would not sink and on 9th May was taken in tow by HMS *Yarmouth*. However, the weather deteriorated and water entered HMS *Sheffield's* hull. The following day she turned over and sank within twenty minutes.

DPR (N) M.o.D.

THE NEW *SHEFFIELD*

The new HMS *Sheffield,* one of the latest design of the Type 22 Frigates, is pictured at her launching ceremony in March 1986. She was launched by Mrs Susan Stanley, wife of the Armed Forces Minister, Mr John Stanley. HMS *Sheffield* was the first Royal Navy ship to be launched, having the same name as a vessel sunk in the Falklands war.

Notable among the guests, as she was sent down the slipway at Swan Hunter Shipbuilder's yard on the Tyne, was Commodore Sam Salt, who as Captain was Commanding Officer of the Type 42 Destroyer bearing the same name, when she was hit by an Argentine Exocet missile. He said that the launch was a poignant moment for all who were linked with his ship and memories would not fade. ''But here we see a new *Sheffield* and the important thing is to look to the future.''

AIRTECH LIMITED

PEGLER-HATTERSLEY plc

DIDSBURY ENGINEERING CO LTD

HMS *SHEFFIELD* MOVES DOWN THE SLIPWAY

The picture shows the new HMS *Sheffield* entering the waters of the River Tyne at Swan Hunter Shipbuilder's Yard, less than four years after her immediate predecessor had been the first warship casualty suffered by the Royal Navy in the Falklands conflict.

New methods of construction at Swan Hunters have reduced the time taken to build new frigates by almost a year. Massive sections of the new HMS *Sheffield* and *Coventry* were prefabricated under-cover before being transferred to the building site on the slipway. Miles of cabling and piping were installed in the prefabricated sections before they were moved to the ships and many compartments were even fully painted.

The experience gained in the Falklands has dictated a change in certain materials used in the building of warships. The PVC cable insulation, which gave off dense smoke and toxic fumes after the previous *Sheffield* was hit has been replaced with new materials that do not give off so much smoke and fumes in a fire. Plastic sheeting has been firmly secured to parts of the ship's superstructure to minimise the risk of splintering under attack.

On the current building timetable, the new HMS *Sheffield* is expected to be ready for acceptance by the Royal Navy towards the end of 1988.

STONE BOILERS — A DIVISION OF
STONE INTERNATIONAL plc

A SHUDDER – AND DOWN THE SLIPWAY GOES THE NEW CONVENTRY.

HMS *COVENTRY*

At 03.45 on 8th April 1986, twelve hours ahead of her scheduled launch, the new HMS *Coventry* slipped her shackles and was sent down Swan Hunter's slipway at Wallsend, by management and staff.

The hush-hush operation was organised to prevent the new Type 22 Frigate's launch being delayed due to a strike over pay by 2,000 boiler-makers and outfitters at the yard. The problem was added to by a forecast of gale-force winds for the following day. In spite of the event occurring in the small hours, the ship was launched, as planned, by Lady Stanford, wife of Admiral Sir Peter Stanford, Commander-in-Chief, Naval Home Command.

However, the vessel was not actually named until later the same day, when the guests invited to the scheduled launch could be present. They included relations of the 19 Officers and men who died when the previous HMS *Coventry*, a Type 42 Destroyer, was sunk by Argentine bombs during the Falklands conflict, four years earlier.

HMS *Coventry* is the sixth of the 'stretched' Type 22 Frigates and is armed with Exocet anti-ship missiles and the Sea Wolf surface-to-air missile system. Like her sister ships, she has the capability of carrying two Lynx helicopters and will also be able to operate a Sea King or the proposed EH 101 medium helicopter. She is the fifth Royal Navy ship to bear the name *Coventry*.

JANE'S PUBLISHING COMPANY LIMITED

By kind permission of Swan Hunter.

THE NEW HMS *SHEFFIELD* AND HMS *COVENTRY*

Shown in the picture are the new HMS *Sheffield* and *Coventry,* moored together at Swan Hunter Shipbuilder's Yard on the Tyne after their respective launchings.

The new HMS *Sheffield* and HMS *Coventry* are two of the Batch 2 design of the Type 22 Frigates and their immediate sister ships are HMS *Boxer,* HMS *Beaver,* HMS *Brave* and HMS *London.* The Batch 1 ships of the Class are HMS *Broadsword,* HMS *Battleaxe,* HMS *Brilliant* and HMS *Brazen,* the first having been operational since 1979.

Ships of the Batch 2 design have an increased length of 146 metres, and increased beam of 14.7 metres and a greater displacement of 4,166 tonnes, than those of Batch 1. They also have a more advanced weapon fit and are powered by the new Rolls-Royce Spey and Tyne gas turbines. All of the ships have controllable pitch propellers. The ships of this class are the first to be designed to the metric system in the Royal Navy and they are built around a missile armament.

ROLLS-ROYCE plc

A Palaceful of Chaplains: with the Archbishop of Canterbury at Lambeth Palace.

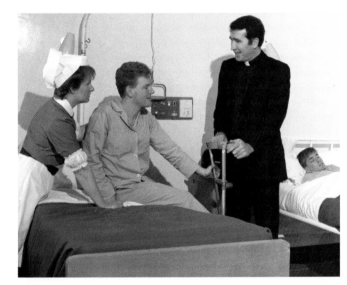

Chaplains at work . . .

TRH The Duke and Duchess of York after their marriage which was assisted by the Venerable Noel Jones.

DPR (N) M.o.D.

ROYAL NAVY CHAPLAINS

Clergymen have gone to sea since the earliest days and the first formal ordering of a Chaplaincy in the Royal Navy dates from the time of Samuel Pepys in the 1670s.

Royal Navy Chaplains represent, within the Service, the Church of England, the Roman Catholic Church, the Church of Scotland and the Free Churches. Other denominations have their Honorary Chaplains. At the present time, just over twenty Royal Navy Chaplains are actually serving at sea. They sail for varying periods of time, from just a week or so, to over nine months at a time, in ships of all sizes from fishery protection vessels to aircraft carriers. All of the principal Royal Navy shore establishments and Naval Air Stations also have their resident Chaplains.

Naval Chaplains have no military rank and thus are free to share in the lives of both sailors and officers. They are first and foremost priests or Ministers of the Church. They care for men and women, both Service and civilian, of a wide age range and from all walks of life, in many different situations. They preach the Word of God and administer the Sacrements; visit the sick and injured; absolve the penitent and counsel the anxious, the bewildered and the bereaved. They prepare men and women for confirmation and marriage and baptise their children. During shore appointments, they set up Sunday Schools, youth clubs and adult study groups.

The Anglican Church in the Royal Navy is, constitutionally, an Archdeaconry of the Diocese of Canterbury, the Archbishop is its Ordinary. Its functional leader has the title "Chaplain of the Fleet", the present holder of that office being the Venerable Noel Jones. There are nearly eighty permanent congregations at home and overseas, ashore and afloat, and others which are dependent upon the number of ships in commission. The Navy's church buildings ashore vary widely, from the magnificent Rococo of the Chapel of the Royal Naval College at Greenwich, to the more modern and practical styles of the newer Naval establishments. It is, however, in its ministry at sea that the Church in the Navy has always been most distinctive, and its history is almost as long as that of the Church itself.

DPR (N) M.o.D.

ROYAL FLEET AUXILIARY REPLENISHMENT VESSEL RFA
FORT VICTORIA

The Royal Fleet Auxiliary Service is the specialist front-line support force for the Royal Navy and its primary task is the replenishment of warships at sea with fuel, stores and weapons. The Fleet currently comprises twenty-nine vessels, including both large and small Fleet tankers, Support tankers, Stores Replenishment ships, Helicopter Support ships, Logistic Landing ships and a Forward Repair ship. Many more are able to operate helicopters and several have hangar facilities. Most of the ships carry self-defensive armament and can operate as integral units of a Naval Task Force. Since its formation in 1905, the RFA has pioneered and perfected the difficult art of Replenishment at Sea (RAS) and is unique in being the only front-line Fleet Service manned by civilian personnel.

A completely new concept to sustaining the Fleet at sea is the Auxiliary Oiler Replenishment Vessel (AOR). Instead of separate tankers carrying fuel and oil and stores ships carrying ammunition and spares, there is to be a "one-stop" replenishment vessel. This will be able to transfer fuel and stores simultaneously to front line ships, whilst steaming alongside. The AOR will also be able to provide maintenance facilities for helicopters.

The "one-stop" concept dates back to 1978 and the first ship of the new class is to be designed and built by Harland and Wolff of Belfast, in conjunction with Yarrow Shipbuilders and Yard. The Government has decided that Swan Hunters should be given a preferential opportunity to bid for the second ship of the class. The new ship will be named RFA *Fort Victoria* and is expected to enter service at about the end of the decade. The new design incorporates many lessons learned from the Falklands Campaign and it will be armed with Seawolf missiles to defend itself and its valuable cargo. Its vulnerability to missile and torpedo attack has been reduced by careful design.

The ship will be large by RFA standards. She will be some 200 metres in length overall and have a beam of around 30 metres. Her displacement will be just over 31,500 tonnes. The ship will be equipped with 4 dual purpose RAS rigs, allowing the simultaneous transfer of liquids and solid stores to the receiving warship, this is the "one-stop" concept. The control centre is sited between the RAS rigs and aft there is a hangar capable of accommodating three EH 101 helicopters, with a flight deck able to accept two aircraft. The ship will be propelled by twin shafts and fixed pitch propellors.

The ship will be crewed with RFA personnel and there will be an RN party embarked. The RFA crew will operate the ship and carry out the RAS operations. The duties of the RN crew will be primarily to maintain and operate the weapons systems and helicopters.

The AOR will be more sophisticated than any other replenishment vessel which has served with the Royal Navy and its method of procurement a prime example of Government policy of devolving the maximum responsibility for the design and procurement of our ships to Industry.

SACCONE & SPEED INTERNATIONAL LTD

THE SEA HARRIER FRS Mark I

The history of the Sea Harrier dates back to the 1950s with the construction of the experimental Rolls-Royce Thrust-Measuring Rig, popularly known as the 'Flying Bedstead' and the revolutionary Hawker P 1127, subsequently named 'The Kestrel'. The Harrier developed directly from the Kestrel and became the world's first "Short Take Off — Vertical Landing" (STOVL) fighter aircraft in 1969. The maritime version evolved in 1975, and after extensive sea trials on HMS *Invincible,* the Royal Navy ordered it as its principal fixed-wing aircraft.

The maritime fighter/reconnaisance/strike Sea Harrier became fully operational in 1980 and is the most advanced ship-borne STOVL aircraft in the world. It is capable of operating from a flight deck without the use of either catapult-assisted take off or arrester-wire landing equipment. The ski-jump launching ramp fitted in the Royal Navy's aircraft carriers greatly improves its operational performance.

Fitted with air interception radar, the Sea Harrier carries a variety of weapons including the Sidewinder air-to-air missile and the Sea Eagle anti-ship missile. The Sea Harrier is a single seat aircraft, it has a length of 14.3 metres, a wingspan of 7.6 metres, a height of 3.6 metres and a speed of over 560 knots. It is powered by a Rolls-Royce Pegasus vectored-thrust turbofan engine.

Three squadrons of Sea Harriers have now been formed and each is represented in the photograph.

DPR (N) M.o.D.

THE TYPE 23 "DUKE CLASS" FRIGATE

HMS *Norfolk,* the first of the new "Duke Class" of frigate is now under construction at Yarrow Shipbuilders and another has been ordered by the Ministry of Defence (Navy). More of this class have been planned and together they will form the backbone of the Royal Navy's frigate replacement programme.

This new class of frigate has been designed by Yarrows (who will also be building two further Type 23s, *(Argyll* and *Lancaster)* primarily for the anti-submarine role and it will be fitted with the latest computerised sonic, radar and communications systems. It will also have a towed array sonar. Air defence will be provided by a vertical launch Sea Wolf weapons system and it will carry a Lynx anti-submarine helicopter and the Sting Ray torpedo. The Lynx helicopter will eventually be replaced by the new EH 101 helicopter, when it comes into service. An all-round surface warfare capability will be provided by the Harpoon missile system and a 114mm automatic rapid-firing gun.

Ships of the new class will have an approximate standard displacement of 3,500 tonnes and will be 133 metres in length with a beam of 14.4 metres. They will carry a complement of 170 officers and men.

YARROW SHIPBUILDERS LTD